AMERICAN ARTILLERY

AMERICAN ARTILLERY

From 1775 to the Present Day

MICHAEL GREEN

Pen & Sword
MILITARY

First published in Great Britain in 2021 by
PEN & SWORD MILITARY
an imprint of
Pen & Sword Books Ltd
47 Church Street
Barnsley
South Yorkshire
S70 2AS

ISBN 978-1-52677-666-2

Typeset by Concept, Huddersfield, West Yorkshire HD4 5JL.
Printed and bound in the UK by CPI Group (UK) Ltd, Croydon, CR0 4YY.

Pen & Sword Books Limited incorporates the imprints of Atlas, Archaeology, Aviation, Discovery, Family History, Fiction, History, Maritime, Military, Military Classics, Politics, Select, Transport, True Crime, Air World, Frontline Publishing, Leo Cooper, Remember When, Seaforth Publishing, The Praetorian Press, Wharncliffe Local History, Wharncliffe Transport, Wharncliffe True Crime and White Owl.

For a complete list of Pen & Sword titles please contact
PEN & SWORD BOOKS LIMITED
47 Church Street, Barnsley, South Yorkshire S70 2AS, England
E-mail: enquiries@pen-and-sword.co.uk
Website: www.pen-and-sword.co.uk

Contents

Dedication

The author dedicates this book to US Army Medal of Honor winner First Lieutenant John R. Fox. His citation reads:

> Commencing with a heavy barrage of enemy artillery at 0400 hours on 26 December 1944, an organized attack by uniformed German units began. Being greatly outnumbered, most of the United States Infantry forces were forced to withdraw from the town, but Lieutenant Fox and some other members of his observer party voluntarily remained on the second floor of a house to direct defensive artillery fire. At 0800 hours, Lieutenant Fox reported that the Germans were in the streets and attacking in strength. He then called for defensive artillery fire to slow the enemy advance. As the Germans continued to press the attack towards the area that Lieutenant Fox occupied, he adjusted the artillery fire closer to his position. Finally, he was warned that the next adjustment would bring the deadly artillery right on top of his position. After acknowledging the danger, Lieutenant Fox insisted that the last adjustment be fired as this was the only way to defeat the attacking soldiers. Later, when a counterattack retook the position from the Germans, Lieutenant Fox's body was found with the bodies of approximately 100 German soldiers.

Foreword

The latest book by Michael Green is a crisp, authoritative work, culled from US Army periodicals and reference material; Green takes us on a different type of history, covering a chronology, production requirements versus military needs, the use and misuse of artillery, and tactical doctrine versus operational performance. Add to this the many varied weapons, systems, tubes, ammunition and associated support vehicles laid out for the reader in well-written essays; the author takes the reader from the first use of artillery in the 1300s to its modern-day place as the 'King of Battle'.

American Artillery begins with a historical essay on the beginnings and use of artillery leading up to the Revolutionary War. Fraught with attempts at standardization, facing tight budgets and political infighting, Green lays out the military requirements and military transport systems leading through the Mexican-American War and just before the Civil War.

Chapter Two brings us through the Civil War and analyzes both the Union and Confederate Army's use and limitations throughout the war. This chapter is chock full of weapon systems: Napoleon cannon, Parrot rifles, James rifle, Armstrong, Whitworth, Blakely cannons, siege and Wiard artillery, and the introduction of mortars and rockets. Each system is evaluated on its effectiveness and problems in combat and production. Additionally, the author brings tube material into the discussion, weighing the effectiveness of bronze, steel, iron, wrought iron and rifled versus smoothbore cannon tubes.

Chapter Three brings us from a constabulary army on the American frontier through the First World War when an untrained and unequipped American Army went to France and underwent training on French artillery systems. This was the age of hurricane bombardments and the nadir of operational military thought, of organization and reorganization, and larger and larger artillery systems.

Chapter Four takes the reader through the planning to raise an army and learn from the operational advances made in Europe by the French, British and Germans during the inter-war period, the Spanish Civil War and into the beginnings of the Second World War.

There was much to learn, from systems to employment, through organization and doctrine, and adding advanced technology to give the infantry soldier a reliable support weapon in the field. Advancements included the proximity fuse and the operational inclusion of 'time on target' against enemy forces. Additionally, technology brought forth self-propelled howitzers, and rockets launched from tanks and trucks and air defense artillery.

Chapters Five and Six, taken together, show the promise and performance of technological advances in the research centers and in the field. Nuclear rounds, tactical nuclear weapons, missiles and integrated systems showed their promise and failures. Through the Cold War, through Operation DESERT STORM and current warfare in the Middle East, systems planners are working on future systems while engaged in current operations, and sometimes actually aiding war-fighters in the field. While the author points out brilliant advances (Paladin, M109A7) he also points out dismal failures (Crusader, Future Combat System), and this is the strength of all his books, including this one.

Finally, there is enough operational information to please the armchair general, enough technical information and accompanying photographs to aid the modeler, and enough detailed information to assist the gamer and re-enactor. Additionally, the author gives military historians a great read and a great primer on the historical development of artillery and pertinent source material for further research.

Randy R. Talbot
Command Historian (Retired)
US Army Tank-automotive and Armaments
Command (TACOM)

Acknowledgements

The historical images in this work come from the files of the National Archives, various US Army Museums, the Department of Defense (DOD) and public domain sites. Some of the contemporary photographs come from US Army and Marine Corps websites. Other pictures came from friends that are named. As with all published works, authors depend on friends for assistance in reviewing their work.

Notes to the Reader

1. Due to the book's size and format, this work is only a very broad overview of the history of American artillery.
2. The US Army eventually began designating its cannons and their carriages separately. The author has chosen only to use the cannon designations in this work.
3. Due to space constraints, the author has not included US Army anti-tank artillery.
4. Sources can vary on the numbers built of artillery pieces, their weight and maximum ranges. Ranges themselves can vary depending on the type of round fired, weather, temperature, etc.

Chapter One

The Early Years

The first written mention of gunpowder artillery in a European document appeared in 1326. At around the same time, the first illustrations of artillery pieces appeared in a manuscript titled *On the Majesty, Wisdom and Prudence of Kings*.

It was civilian contractors, not soldiers, who operated early cannons. As the cannons lacked sufficient mobility, they tended to be fixed in position before a battle or siege began and did not move again until the conclusion of the fighting. The demand for mobile artillery, therefore, drove metallurgical experimentation and advances.

French King Charles VIII (1483–98) commissioned horse-drawn lightweight artillery pieces mounted on two-wheeled carriages. In contrast, the armies of other European kingdoms depended on large cannons affixed to wooden sleds fitted with solid wooden wheels and pulled by draft animals such as oxen. The mobility advantage enjoyed by Charles's army allowed it to prevail on many a battlefield.

Despite the many advancements introduced by the French artillery branch during Charles VIII's reign, Charles's army still lacked the tactical and organizational skills for maneuvering its artillery pieces after the first cannonade between opposing sides.

A Swedish King makes Improvements

Gustavus Adolphus, the King of Sweden (1611–32), improved his artillery by placing military officers in charge of the civilian contractors. They, in turn, constantly drilled the civilian contractors to improve their speed and accuracy on the battlefield.

Under Gustavus Adolphus' oversight, the Swedish Army mastered the tactical and organizational skills necessary for maneuvering field artillery pieces into the most advantageous firing positions as a battle evolved. This skill set was never mastered by Charles VIII's artillery branch. Gustavus also divided his artillery pieces into two different self-explanatory types: 'field' and 'siege'. He is consideeed by some to be the father of modern field artillery.

In the early 1440s, individual artillery types went by different names, typically animals or birds of prey. Early cannons were often highly embellished and marked with inscriptions. On French cannons, the inscription ordered by King Louis XIV (1643–1715) read *'Ultima Ratio Regum'* ('the final argument of kings').

New Tactical Roles

The next tactical development began by Frederick the Great, King of Prussia (1740–86). He mounted his field artillery crews on saddle horses so that they could maintain pace with the cavalry. With this enhanced mobility, they kept up with and supported the king's cavalry, as well as infantry units, as they maneuvered on the battlefield. The arrangement became known as 'horse artillery'. Cannon crews who walked alongside their towed artillery pieces became known as 'foot artillery'.

Frederick's horse artillery could successfully engage massed enemy infantry formations because their smoothbore cannons outranged their opponents' smoothbore muskets. The German king's battlefield accomplishments prompted the British and French armies to also adopt the horse artillery system, the former in 1792 and the latter in 1793.

Napoleon's Artillery

Napoleon Bonaparte (1769–1821), originally an artillery officer, dominated the battlefields of the Napoleonic Wars (1803–15) by massing his horse artillery batteries, as had Frederick the Great. Napoleon stated that 'God fights on the side with the best artillery.' As during Frederick's reign, Napoleon's smoothbore cannons outranged the smoothbore muskets used by his enemies.

French horse artillerymen, according to French baron and military officer Joseph Seruzier (1769–1823), 'were renowned for their courage, and no less for their contentious spirit. They pushed 'esprit de corps' far beyond the point of virtue and believed themselves infinitely superior to their comrades in the foot artillery.'

Other European kingdoms also adopted the horse artillery system with variations. As a result of the high cost of maintaining horse artillery (and the horses, training, forage, fodder, grooming, veterinary services, etc.), most countries also continued to deploy foot artillery as it was more affordable.

US Army Labels

The US Army would use the term 'light artillery' in place of foot artillery. Beginning before the American Civil War, the label light artillery eventually found itself replaced by the title of 'mounted artillery'.

The Match is Lit

To recoup some of the cost of the French and Indian War (1754–63), the British government taxed British colonists residing in the thirteen colonies located along the Atlantic Coast of what later became the United States. The colonists' resentment aroused by these and other taxes led to bitter protest and escalating events.

The final episode that resulted in what became the Revolutionary War (1775–83) began when a British Army detachment set out from Boston,

---

Some Artillery Definitions

A 'limber' is a two-wheeled cart attached to the 'trail' end of the two-wheeled carriage of an artillery piece and first appeared in 1453. The limber converted an artillery piece into a four-wheeled trailer. The trail is that part of a gun carriage that extends rearward from the axle to reach the ground, so when lowered, the barrel remains level. It also supports the weight of a cannon barrel and aids in resisting the recoil shock when firing the weapon.

The term 'cannon' is a generic name for all tube artillery pieces. A 'gun' is typically an artillery piece with a long tube, a high muzzle velocity and a flat trajectory below 45 degrees. 'Muzzle velocity' is the speed of a cannonball (also referred to as shot or shell) upon leaving a cannon tube. The trajectory is the cannonball's path as it flies through the air.

Falling into the siege artillery category was the 'mortar', invented by the Turks in 1457. From a US Army manual is a description of mortars: '... cannons with short, usually smoothbore, barrels and with very low muzzle velocities. They are almost always fired at very steep elevations.' Most definitions of mortars describe the weapons as designed only to fire at angles greater than 45 degrees. Mortars were labeled, starting in the seventeenth century, by the diameter of their bore in inches.

In the 1690s, the Dutch developed the 'howitzer'. The French Army had its first howitzer made in 1749. Like the mortar, howitzers find themselves described by the diameter of their bore in inches. A US Army manual defines a howitzer as a 'comparatively short cannon with a medium muzzle velocity. Howitzers are usually fired at relatively steep elevations so the rounds can reach targets hidden from flat-trajectory guns. Variations in the propelling charge change a round's trajectory and range. The howitzer's range lies between the gun and the mortar.'

Massachusetts on the morning of April 19, 1775. Their assignment: to arrest a rebel colonist leader in the town of Lexington and seize gunpowder collected by colonial rebels at the town of Concord.

Alerted to the British Army plans by spies, armed rebel colonists confronted the British soldiers on Lexington Green. Following the initial encounter, a series of running gun battles followed with the reinforced British detachment repulsed with heavy losses.

The rebels knew there was no turning back and began preparations for war with the British Empire. Besides calling up all available militia units for training, the rebel colonial leadership began collecting all the weaponry that could be located, including cannons.

The American Experience with Artillery

On May 19, 1775 the legislature of the colony of Massachusetts organized an artillery regiment under the command of Colonel Richard Gridley. He had gained fame for his handling of artillery during the French and Indian War while in the service of the British Army.

As with contemporary British Army practice, the Massachusetts artillery regiment was an administrative entity. It oversaw up to eight or more companies, each having anywhere from two to six artillery pieces.

On June 14, 1775, the representatives from the thirteen British colonies, known as the Continental Congress, voted to authorize the formation of the Continental Army. General George Washington was appointed its commander-in-chief. He would also oversee all the various volunteer state militia units. Colonel Gridley became the chief of artillery for the Continental Army.

The First Artillery Battle

The British government believed that suppression of the port city of Boston in the Massachusetts Colony would quell the rebellion and so invested the city with land and naval forces early in 1775. The colonial militia set up breastworks outside the city but was unable to challenge the British regulars with musketry alone. To supplement their firepower, the colonists brought in six cannons.

Name Changes

Eventually, the label 'company' concerning American artillery units would find itself replaced by the term 'battery' during the build-up preceding the Mexican-American War (1846–48). The 'word' battery comes from its historical role: 'to batter down' the walls of fortresses.

Colonel Gridley, a supposedly experienced military engineer, designed the earthen and wood defensive works for the colonists but failed to provide either raised firing platforms or embrasures for the artillery pieces. Upon their arrival, the artillerymen had to blast gaps through the existing earthworks to create fields of fire for their weapons.

The British Army marched out of Boston to take Breed Hill on June 17, 1775 in what became known as the Battle of Bunker Hill. Enduring a great many casualties during two failed attempts to capture the colonists' defensive lines, the British launched a successful third assault, as the rebel colonists had largely run out of ammunition.

The British captured five of the colonists' six artillery pieces. Colonel Gridley, present at Breed Hill that day, was wounded during the fighting. Two of the captains overseeing the rebel colonists' artillery came up on charges of cowardice for deserting their posts during the fighting, one of them a son of Colonel Gridley.

The Next Stage

On arriving at the colonists' defensive positions located on the outskirts of Boston during July 1775, General Washington removed the 64-year-old Gridley from his artillery post for incompetence. Gridley would retain the title of chief engineer of the Continental Army until 1781. The first two men to whom Washington offered Gridley's former job passed, as they felt they were too old for the demands of the position.

On November 17, 1775, a young Boston bookseller named Henry Knox offered to assist Washington in artillery matters. He had been at Breed Hill on the day of battle and had read books on the subject of artillery. He had also received some hands-on artillery training from British Army instructors in the 1760s during the French and Indian War. Knox was made a colonel in the Continental Army artillery.

Knox's Influence Grows

Having greatly impressed Washington, Knox recommended that the amount of artillery available for the ongoing siege lacked the required numbers; he proposed that cannons captured in May by the colonists at Fort Ticonderoga be moved 300 miles overland to Boston to strengthen the siege. Despite the obvious difficulty, Washington approved.

Upon reaching Fort Ticonderoga in December, Knox selected fifty-nine artillery pieces of varying sizes. Using sleds pulled by oxen, and barges, Knox had the artillery pieces delivered and emplaced in firing positions on Dorchester Heights, which commanded the city, the harbor and British defenses, by March 2, 1776. The British Army commander quickly realized his defensive positions were now untenable and withdrew from Boston by sea for Halifax, Canada on March 17, 1775.

Washington and Knox would continue to review and revise their ideas on the proper employment of artillery throughout the Revolutionary War, based on lessons learned on the battlefield as well as the latest European trends. Knox emphasized to the army's artillerymen that on the battlefield, they concentrate their fire on enemy infantry formations rather than enemy artillery pieces.

Helping the Infantry

By early August 1776, Washington and Knox had decided to add light-weight field artillery pieces to the Continental Army's infantry formations. These would include 3- and 6-pounder cannons, labeled as 'battalion guns'. Knox, however, preferred the French light artillery 4-pounder, but ammunition for the two other cannon sizes was more readily available. The term 'pounder' referred to the approximate weight of a solid cannon-ball fired from its respective artillery piece.

Washington and Knox believed that the addition of field artillery pieces to their infantry units would stiffen their resolve on the battlefield. Unfortunately, combat experience quickly demonstrated that a lack of trained artillerymen reduced the weapons' effectiveness. To help rectify this situation, Washington and Knox began recruiting experienced artillerymen from France and the Netherlands.

Improving the Artillery

As the Continental Army had difficulty acquiring locally-produced cannons for their needs, foreign weapons, especially French, were purchased. Knox saw this dependence on foreign weapons and the artillerymen to operate them as a short-term measure only. Knox would become the chief of artillery of the Continental Army at the end of 1776, receiving a promotion to major general in 1782.

Knox tried with limited success to push the Continental Congress to fund new artillery units. He also wanted to establish artillery schools and arsenals to provide the trained manpower and weapons required to make the Continental Army less dependent on overseas sources, but without success.

In late 1776, the Continental Congress finally began to enlarge the Continental Army, including three regiments of artillery, eventually increased to four. Each would contain field artillery, siege artillery and garrison artillery, the last for defending fortifications. Washington and Knox did

Bronze or Cast Iron

From a US Army historical publication titled *The Organizational History of Field Artillery 1776–2003* by author Janice E. Mokenney is this passage describing the materials employed in making cannons:

> Most cannons in American service during the Revolutionary War were made of bronze [known as brass at the time], with the exception of the largest: the 32-pounder gun. Bronze was more resistant to corrosion and metal fatigue. The only limitation was the short supply of the constituent elements of copper and nickel, foreign metals that had to be imported into America. Bronze cannons were lighter than iron, which made them more maneuverable in the field. For siege weapons or for those in permanent fortifications, where weight was not an issue, cast iron was more often used.

not rule out employing field artillery pieces in the siege artillery role if required.

During the winter of 1777–78, French artillery experts were brought into the country to bring the standard of training of Continental Army artillerymen up to an acceptable level in Knox's view. At the same time, he decided to revamp the army's artillery inventory by standardization. It involved reducing the number of different sizes of artillery pieces to simplify the logistical and training system in imitation of European practices.

From fifteen different calibers in the field artillery category, Knox's efforts at standardization brought it down to seven, and in the siege artillery category, the number of calibers went from twelve to seven. The term 'caliber' refers to the inside diameter of a cannon's bore, and in more modern times also as a measure of a cannon's length. To improve flexibility, Knox had all his artillerymen cross-trained on the various types of artillery in the inventory.

Positive Results

Knox's continued efforts to upgrade the Continental Army's artillery branch paid off during the Battle of Monmouth in New Jersey on June 28, 1778. Despite the fighting eventually proving inconclusive, the Continental Army's artillery, in conjunction with the infantry, demonstrated that they could engage in conventional battle and hold their own against the British Army. A Continental Army artillerist present at the battle later recalled in his journal, 'Our troops behaved with the greatest bravery, and opposed the flower of the British Army. Our artillery was well served and did amazing execution.'

With the help of the French, who had declared war on Great Britain on March 17, 1778, the tide of battle soon turned in favor of the United States. The closing event of the conflict occurred during the Siege of Yorktown (September 28–October 19, 1781).

The Yorktown siege was the last major land battle ending with a French fleet offshore, and the British Army located within the town pounded into submission by Continental Army and French siege artillery. An official peace treaty between the United States and the British Empire went in effect on September 3, 1783.

That Knox was able to create an artillery force equal to that of the British Army in the span of just a few years from almost nothing was noted by the Marquis de Lafayette, a French military officer. He would remark, 'The progress of [American] artillery during the Revolution was regarded by all conversant with the facts as one of the wonders of that interesting period.'

Early Indian Wars

With the end of the Revolutionary War, American settlers began pushing westward into an area south of the Great Lakes and north of the Ohio River. The Native American tribes in that region banded together, with the unofficial support of local British traders, to launch raids against the American settlers.

The Continental Army had, by this time, shrunk from its wartime high of approximately 80,000 men to a force of fewer than 1,000 men. Congress did not trust large standing armies and was desperately short of money following the Revolutionary War. As a stop-gap measure, it decided to authorize the enlistment of untrained militiamen to reinforce the small force of regular troops tasked with stopping the Native American raids. The army's remaining artillery pieces and men became 'The Battalion of Artillery', a title in place from 1789 until 1791.

The fighting between the American military forces and the Native Americans following the Revolutionary War was called the North-West Indian War (1785–95). Due to humiliating defeats at the hands of the Native Americans in both 1790 and 1791, Congress disbanded what remained of the Continental Army and created a new army labeled as the Legion of the United States in 1792.

The Legion consisted of a standing army of approximately 5,000 men, including infantry, cavalry and artillery units, and based upon the former Continental Army and a large number of recruits. The Legion was composed of four sub-legions, each supported by an artillery battery armed with 6-pounder guns and 3in and 5.5in howitzers.

After rigorous training in 1783, the Legion began campaigning in the spring of 1794. Its senior leadership strongly believed in the contribution that could be made by field artillery, so it brought along a few 3in howitzers. These small weapons' advantage was that they broke down into separate components that could be carried by individual pack animals. The label 'mountain artillery' and eventually 'pack artillery' was eventually attached to such cannons.

The US Army Appears

The Legion's campaign of 1794 concluded with victory over the Native Americans at the Battle of Fallen Timbers in what is now the state of Ohio, on August 20, 1794. Despite unfavorable terrain conditions, the 3in howitzers did play a part in the fighting. In 1796, the Legion officially became the 'Army of the United States', hereafter referred to as the 'US Army'.

From 1794 up through the early 1800s, the majority of US Army officers operating along the Western Frontier of the United States believed that field artillery was more trouble than it was worth. However, on occasion it did prove useful, as appears in these passages from a government publication titled *Field Artillery in Military Operations Other than War: An Overview of the US Experience*:

> In the course of over a century of Indian warfare, there were numerous occasions on which artillery fire repelled or dispersed an organized attack by hostile bands against an Army fort. Often, the firing of an artillery round or two, or even the mere presence of the guns, had enough of a psychological impact on natives unfamiliar with weaponry beyond small arms to deter an attack or to frighten off the attackers with few or no casualties on either side.

Name Changes

With ever-rising tensions between the French and British, beginning as early as 1792, there arose a concern among many Americans that the United States might become involved in the fighting on one side or the other. In response, Congress formed in 1794 a new artillery organization labeled the 'Corps of Artillery and Engineers'; its task was building and eventually manning twenty-one seacoast artillery defensive fortifications along the Atlantic Coast of the United States. A bit later, there appeared a second organization labeled the 'Regiment of Artillery and Engineers'.

In 1798, the Corps of Artillery and Engineers became the US Army's 'First Artillery Regiment' and the Regiment of Artillery and Engineers the US Army's 'Second Artillery Regiment'. All the various name changes did not hide the fact that compared to its European counterparts, the US Army remained fairly unsophisticated in its use of artillery.

Trying to Improve

It was the American Secretary of War, James McHenry (1796–1800), that pushed for another much-needed round of modernization of the US Army's inventory of both field and seacoast artillery. Just before leaving office, he began to stress the importance of the US Army adopting horse artillery.

McHenry also pushed for schools to create professional artillerymen, as had his predecessor, Henry Knox. Sadly, none of his ideas bore fruit as Congress was short of the necessary funding and, at the same time, feared a professional full-time officer corps.

McHenry's replacement as Secretary of War was Henry Dearborn (1801–9). He, like his predecessors, kept trying to upgrade the US Army's artillery inventory. Dearborn hired a French artillery expert, Louis de Tousard, to help. Tousard's main goal, along with Dearborn's, was to streamline the inventory by reducing the number of field gun models from three sizes of bronze construction down to only one, an iron 6-pounder.

Tousard and Dearborn knew that cast-iron cannons were not as durable as bronze cannons, but iron was readily available in the United States whereas bronze was not. Also the quality of cast-iron cannon manufacturing had improved due to continuing developments in the field of metallurgy.

Iron cannon made sense to many and, as a result, the US Army ceased employing bronze cannons in 1801 and did not employ them again until 1836. The army changed its mind due to concerns expressed by field artillerymen on the safety of cast-iron cannons. A then survey of modern European artillery practices confirmed that bronze cannons remained superior to the existing cast-iron cannons.

Despite Dearborn's and Tousard's efforts, President Thomas Jefferson (1801–9) and Congress refused to fund most of their suggestions. In 1802, due to the easing of war fears, the president and Congress reduced the size of the US Army in its latest reorganization and put Tousard out of a job. At the same time, the US Army's engineers found themselves separated from what became known as the 'Regiment of Artillery'. The regiment was reclassified as the 'Corps of Artillery' in 1814.

More War

In 1808, Congress tripled the size of the US Army as fear of becoming involved in the Napoleonic Wars (1803–15) grew among Americans once again. Dearborn used the occasion to press for the adoption of horse artillery to support the cavalry by forming a demonstration battery in 1808.

Despite the demonstration battery's impressive performance, it was considered too costly to maintain, which led to its disbanding in 1809. The artillerymen who had formed the demonstration battery went off to sea-coast artillery units or to serve on the Western Frontier, guarding forts against attacks by Native Americans.

The United States finally became involved in the Napoleonic conflicts by declaring war on Great Britain in June 1812 in what became known as the 'War of 1812'. Despite all the efforts made up to that time in trying to improve its artillery inventory and training, the US Army still lacked an adequate number of qualified artillerymen as well as modern artillery pieces.

With the beginning of the War of 1812, the American War Department authorized the creation of horse-drawn 'light artillery' batteries. This idea proved difficult to implement due to a shortage of both cannons and horse, leading most light artillery batteries serving as infantry during the war.

The actual fighting between the US and British armies led to victories and defeats on both sides. In two rather large battles, at Chippewa in July 1814 and New Orleans in January 1815, a more experienced US Army artillery branch dominated their British Army counterparts.

General Andrew Jackson, a future American president (1829–37), credited his artillery with a very decisive part in turning back the British Army at the Battle of New Orleans. That thought appears in this quote attributed to him: 'Too much praise cannot be bestowed on those who managed my artillery.'

A New Chapter

In 1815, following the War of 1812, Congress once again reduced the US Army's size. Colonel Decius Wadsworth, chief of the newly-founded US Army Ordnance Department, was not pleased. He pressed Congress to release the funding necessary to keep the army's artillery inventory up to date.

In 1820, Congress decided once again to reduce the size of the US Army. It would drop from 10,000 men down to 6,000. The Corps of Artillery, the Light Artillery Regiment and the Ordnance Department were all folded into four regiments of artillery, each consisting of nine batteries. One of those nine batteries in each regiment was to be horse artillery, although there were never enough horses available to make this a reality.

Seacoast Artillery

With the 1820 reorganization of the artillery branch, Congress put aside funding for the construction of both new seacoast artillery fortifications as well as the rebuilding of older-generation examples. Before the American Civil War, seacoast artillery was considered the country's first line of defense, resulting in far more seacoast artillery pieces in service than field artillery pieces.

Seacoast artillery was considered heavy artillery, but distinct from siege and garrison artillery as it would be found typically only in fixed defensive fortifications. As the requirement for movement would not be a consideration in seacoast artillery designs, they would prove to be much larger and heavier than their siege and garrison artillery counterparts.

Trying to Decide

In 1831, the Secretary of War, Lewis Cass (1831–36), wrote to President Andrew Jackson out of concern that the US Army Artillery Branch lacked the weapons necessary to defend the country from foreign aggression.

A board of senior officers was organized in 1835 and 1839 to determine the best methods to redress the issue. One important choice was made: bronze was a better choice than cast-iron for field artillery pieces.

In 1838, Secretary of War Joel Poinsett (1837–41) ordered the forming of a battery of light artillery from the men of the 1st and 2nd Artillery Regiments. The following year he then ordered the forming of three more batteries of light artillery. However, the War Department countermanded the second order.

Poinsett was keenly aware that there were serious shortcomings with the US Army's artillery inventory and training system, which he pointed out in reports to the War Department. To address the training issue, Poinsett organized one-year training camps for artillery batteries in which they could drill together.

Poinsett created an ordnance board in 1839. It, in turn, assigned Alfred Mordecai, a well-respected captain of ordnance, to design on paper a new artillery system. Secretary of War George W. Crawford (1849–50) gave his

---

Garrison Artillery

Garrison artillery typically consisted of field artillery pieces mounted onto smaller and more compact four-wheeled carriages, similar to those employed on naval warships, allowing for them to line the often-narrow ramparts of defensive structures such as castles.

Muzzle-Loading Ammunition

Artillery pieces originally fired solid spherical balls made of stone, also referred to as 'cannonballs'. However, by the 1450s, these were replaced by spherical balls made of solid cast-iron. These were referred to by several somewhat similar names, which included 'shot', 'round shot', 'solid shot' and 'ball'.

The solid cast-iron balls (falling under the category of cannonballs) were attached to a wooden 'sabot' by tin straps which allowed for ease of loading. The sabot was used to prevent damage to the bore of brass cannons and ensure that the fuze of a shell remained in or near the axis of the piece.

Behind the sabot and attached to it was the 'charge', hereafter referred to as the 'propelling charge'. The three components together formed a complete round of ammunition, referred to as 'fixed'. When a projectile and propelling charge went into a cannon separately, the round became known as 'semi-fixed'. Fixed ammunition became the preferred cannon ammunition by the 1840s for its ease of handling, speed of loading and reduction in loading errors.

Shot was extremely effective against massed formations of infantry and cavalry at ranges over 350 yards. As an added advantage when striking the ground, shot would sometimes ricochet a certain distance, creating collateral damage. Another use for shot was to batter down enemy defensive fortifications.

Eventually supplementing inert shot for smoothbore cannons were two types of explosive rounds referred to as 'spherical case' and 'spherical shell'. Typically, both were simply referred to as 'case shot', and when fired from rifled cannons it became known as a 'shell'. They were hollow cast-iron rounds containing a bursting charge with timed fuzes set to detonate at a certain height over a target, showering them with varying numbers of lead or iron balls or fragments.

For massed infantry formation at ranges from approximately 500 to 1,500 yards, spherical case (also referred to as shrapnel) was the round of choice; for shorter ranges there appeared 'canister'. The maximum range of the round was approximately 400 yards, but it was most effective at 100 to 200 yards. It consisted of a tin cylinder containing iron or lead balls packed in dry sawdust. On occasion, two canister rounds went into the cannons when the targets (enemy infantry or cavalry) were extremely close. A 12-pounder canister for the civil war Napoleon cannon contained twenty-seven iron balls while a 12-pounder howitzer canister round contained forty-eight iron balls.

approval in 1849 for the implementation of Mordecai's recommended field artillery system. It consisted of 6- and 12-pounder guns and 12-, 24- and 32-pounder howitzers, as well as a 12-pounder mountain howitzer.

War with Mexico

Ongoing border disputes between the United States and Mexico led to the Mexican-American War (1846–48). Despite the Mexican Army possessing a larger number of troops, the US Army proved better trained and its officers possessed a higher level of competence than their opponents. US Army artillery would prove to be a key force multiplier during the conflict.

Three days before the war was made official by Congress, the US Army, under the command of Major General Zachary Taylor, fought a battle with the Mexican Army on May 8, 1846: the Battle of Palo Alto. The engagement occurred on a treeless plain located within what are now the city limits of Brownsville, Texas.

From a US Army Center of Military History publication titled *Guns Along the Rio Grande: Palo Alto and Resaca de la Palma* is this extract comparing the US Army's and Mexican Army's artillery:

> From the onset, it was clear that the US artillery would dominate on the open field of battle, if only because the Mexicans' copper cannons lacked the necessary range to be effective. Their iron round shot often fell short of their targets and bounced slowly toward Taylor's men. By contrast, the American guns were updated 1840 model weapons with a range of 1,500 yards and could be reloaded quickly.

Not a big believer in the value of field artillery before the Mexican-American War, General Taylor changed his mind after the Battle of Palo Alto. He would state that '... to the excellent manner in which it [horse artillery] was maneuvered and served is our success mainly due.'

The Mexican Army's commanding general learned a painful lesson during the Battle of Palo Alto on the vulnerability of his cavalry and infantry to the well-handled US Army horse artillery. The latter was referred to as the 'flying artillery' at that time.

The Fighting Continues

A second engagement, the Battle of Resaca de la Palma, took place on May 9, 1846, with the Mexican commanding general sheltering his infantry in a thickly-forested area. By doing so, he reduced the ability of the US Army's flying artillery to play a role. Despite that, the Mexican Army suffered another terrible defeat, losing most of its artillery to the US Army.

Between September 21 and 24, 1846, Taylor's army secured most of the Mexican port city of Monterrey, despite being badly outnumbered. In the urban fighting that took place, the lightweight 6- and 12-pounders of his flying artillery were not particularly useful against the city's thick-walled fortifications, a valuable lesson learned by the US Army on the limitations of its existing field artillery. Lacking siege artillery, Taylor depended on a single 10in mortar and two 24-pounder howitzers to support his infantry assaults on the city.

At the Battle of Buena Vista (February 22-23, 1847), Taylor's flying artillery once again had an opportunity to show what it could do on the battlefield against a numerically superior force. Brigadier General John E. Wood, Taylor's second-in-command, would comment, 'without our artillery, we could not have maintained our position for a single hour.'

A New General Enters the Fray

It fell to a second American Army, under the command of Major General Winfield Scott, to force the Mexican government to sue for peace. Scott's first step was to capture the Mexican coastal fortress of Vera Cruz, located on the Gulf of Mexico. Considered one of the best-defended ports in North America, it fell to Scott after a twenty-day siege that lasted from March 9 until March 29, 1847.

Playing an important role in Scott's success at Vera Cruz was an impressive array of US Army siege artillery including guns, howitzers and mortars. In a 1911 article in the *Field Artillery Journal* by Major William J. Snow titled 'The Classification of Field Artillery' he describes siege artillery:

> ... it is generally understood that such artillery comprises guns, howitzers, mortars, etc., that are not permanently horsed and which do not normally accompany an army but which are brought up when needed for some specific purpose...and that when the guns are placed in position, they generally stay there until the siege is over.

Rockets

A new weapon placed into service with the US Army during the siege of Vera Cruz was the rocket. The War Department thought that the US Army's artillerymen lacked the experience to operate the weapon in battle. It, therefore, passed the use of the rockets to the men of the US Army Ordnance Department, who had fired them during testing. The performance of the rockets in combat proved disappointing.

From Vera Cruz, Scott pushed his army toward Mexico's capital, Mexico City. After taking intervening Mexican Army defensive positions as well as defeating large Mexican armies at the Battle of Cerro Gordo (April 18, 1847) and the Battle of Churubusco (August 20, 1847), Scott's army was less than 5 miles away from Mexico City. After waiting for supplies and reinforcements, Scott began his assault on Mexico City on September 8, 1847. His men secured the city on September 15, 1847.

In a report dated September 18, 1847, Scott wrote to Secretary of War William L. Marcy (1845–49) describing the lead-up to the capture of Chapultepec Castle, a defensive position sitting atop a 200-foot (60m) hill on the outskirts of Mexico City:

> To prepare for an assault, it was foreseen that the play of the batteries might run into the second day; but recent captures [Mexican Army artillery] had not only trebled our siege-pieces but also our ammunition, and we knew that we should greatly augment both by carrying the place. I was, therefore, in no haste in ordering an assault before the works were well crippled by our missiles.

Despite the destruction of their armies and the loss of their capital city, the Mexican government did not sign a peace treaty, the Treaty of Guadalupe Hidalgo, until February 2, 1848. Congress ratified the treaty on March 10, 1848. Estimated Mexican casualties during the war, including civilians, were estimated to be around 25,000, with American losses put at approximately 13,300, the majority being military personnel.

Columbiads and Rodmans

The majority of America's pre-Civil War cast-iron seacoast artillery pieces designs came from the keen mind of US Army officer George Bomford (1780–1848). His cannons were all named the 'Columbiad', with his first dedicated anti-ship example appearing in 1811. Bomford's seacoast artillery cannons ranged from a 65-pounder to a 128-pounder, which initially began appearing in service in 1844.

Due to unforeseen design issues during the manufacture of ever-larger cast-iron Columbiad cannons, they proved less reliable and more prone to failure during construction and when fired. US Army officer Thomas J. Rodman (1816–71) overcame that problem before the Civil War by devising a new method of construction which significantly improved their durability.

The War Department approved the building of the first Columbiad cannon under Rodman's new method in 1859. A prototype was successfully trialed in March 1861, leading the US Army to order almost 800 units

Artillery Organization

In John Gibbon's *Artillerist's Manual* from 1860 is the following extract explaining the breakdown of the field artillery branch:

> The following is the most recent division of the United States artillery into kinds according to its duties. Heavy or foot-artillery is that portion which takes charge of and manoeuvres the siege, seacoast, and mountain-artillery. Light or field-artillery, is that portion which manoeuvres field-pieces with troops in the field. It is divided into horse-artillery and mounted batteries. In horse-artillery, the cannoneers, of which there are eleven to each piece, are mounted on horses, from which they have to dismount before attending on the piece, the two extra men holding the horses of the rest. In the mounted batteries, formerly called foot-artillery, the cannoneers are on foot, and remain so during the manoeuvres of the battery, except when it is desired to move at a very rapid rate, when they are mounted on the ammunition-boxes. The horse-artillery was originally and is still designed for service with cavalry, receiving the lightest guns, which enables it to move at the same rate as the cavalry, and to keep it up for a considerable time.

of the Rodman version of the Columbiad cannons. These came in a wide variety of sizes during the American Civil War.

All the Columbiad cannons built using the Rodman process featured a very pronounced glass soda bottle shape, with the breech end of the weapons much thicker than the muzzle end. The names Columbiad and Rodman were often used interchangeably during the Civil War for the cannons.

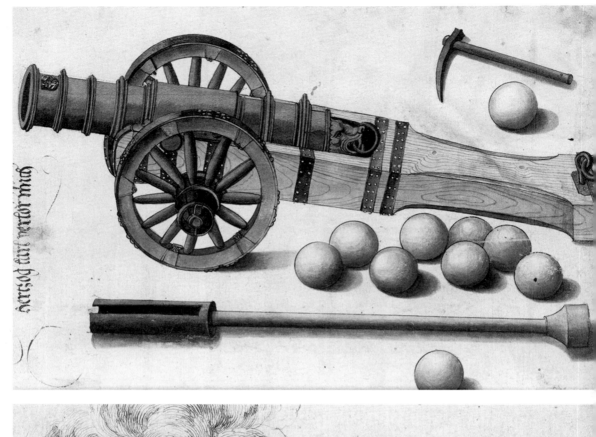

Hertzog kúrt vertor mich

(**Opposite, above**) Due to the poor quality of early gunpowder, stones were the preferred cannon ammunition as they were lighter than iron cannonballs of the same size. The amount of gunpowder required to propel a large iron cannonball would have burst the early cannons. Note the rammer employed to force a cannonball down into the chamber of the weapon, where the propelling charge lay. (*Public domain: PICRYL*)

(**Opposite, below**) In a 1641 illustration we see cannons laying siege to a fortified position. Note how the illustrator has tried to depict the immense amount of smoke generated by firing the weapons. The exact date when gunpowder (also known as black powder) appeared and who discovered it remains unknown. A very unstable compound, it was sensitive to flame and spark, making it extremely dangerous to the cannoneers of all armies. (*PICRYL*)

(**Above**) As time went on and cannon-makers became ever more proficient in their craft, their products became very ornamental, cast with the various symbols of those royal families which commissioned them, as well as inscriptions denoting their owners. Projecting from either side of the cannon's barrel and pictured here are the trunnions which connect the cannon with its carriage and transmit the force of recoil from one to the other. (*PICRYL*)

Gustavus Adolphus, King of Sweden (1611–32), pictured here, following in the footsteps of the French King Charles VIII (1483–98), decided that the best way to improve the battlefield effectiveness of his cannons was to make them more mobile. He also insisted on better-trained artillerymen. The Swedish king died in battle in 1632 and his push to improve artillery fell by the wayside as others lacked his brilliance and drive. (*PICRYL*)

Cannons and the draft animals that towed them onto the battlefield were originally operated by civilian contractors. Not subject to military discipline, they sometimes departed
the battlefield of their own volition. European armies eventually began to form their own
artillery units, beginning with the French in 1693. The artillery officer pictured here has a
short saber as a badge of rank, and possibly for enforcing discipline. (*PICRYL*)

(**Above, left**) Prussian King Frederick the Great (1740–86), pictured here, built on the pioneering efforts of both Charles VIII and Gustavus Adolphus, taking the next big step in increasing the mobility of his field artillery. He did this by mounting some of his light artillerymen on the horses that towed both the cannons and ammunition into battle, creating the first horse artillery units. These he employed with great success in numerous battles. (*PICRYL*)

(**Above, right**) Napoleon Bonaparte (1769–1821,) pictured here, proved to be the next great innovator in tactical employment of artillery. Trained as an artillery officer as a young man, he, like the other great captains before him, strongly believed that massing his artillery pieces in battle under central control and directing their fire at enemy infantry formations would decide many a battle. (*PICRYL*)

(**Opposite, above**) The earliest mortars sat upon wooden platforms and were fixed in elevation. The distance a round flew varied according to the amount of gunpowder used. The example pictured here has a metal platform with trunnions so its elevation could be adjusted. Early mortars found favor as siege weapons as their rounds dropped in a steep arcing trajectory, useful in reaching targets behind defensive walls which flat-trajectory rounds could not. (*PICRYL*)

(**Opposite, below**) An illustration of the so-called Battle of Lexington on April 19, 1775, in which a small group of militiamen confronted a much larger detachment of British Army troops sent out from Boston, Massachusetts, to find any insurrectionists' store of artillery munitions. A shot rang out and the British troops fired on the assembled militiamen, some of whom were killed, with the rest fleeing. It marked the beginning of the American Revolutionary War (1775–87). (*PICRYL*)

Well aware of the dangers inherent in taking on the British Empire's military forces, the colonists quickly set about organizing a government and an army that could defend the thirteen colonies. Appointed head of the Continental Army was George Washington, pictured here, who had gained military experience during the French and Indian War (1754–63) as a colonial militia officer. (*PICRYL*)

In this famous painting we see the British Army troops garrisoned in Boston, Massachusetts, advancing up Breed's Hill (misnamed Bunker Hill) on June 17, 1775 in the face of heavy fire from the besieging colonial militiamen supported by six cannons. It took the British regulars three attempts to dislodge their opponents, triumphing as the American militiamen ran out of ammunition. (*PICRYL*)

Henry Knox, pictured here, is wearing the uniform of a major general of the Continental Army. His original career was that of a book dealer in Boston, Massachusetts. When the American Revolutionary War began, he joined the militia units besieging British-occupied Boston. When General George Washington arrived on scene, he appointed Knox as his chief artillery officer. Knox also served as the first United States Secretary of War from 1789 to 1794. (*PICRYL*)

(**Above**) In this illustration we see the gun crew of a Continental Army cannon. The artilleryman in the foreground is holding a wooden shaft with a sponge at the end to swab clean the barrel's interior after firing. Under the cannon's barrel is a water-filled sponge bucket; the water extinguished any burning embers in the barrel to make safe the loading of the next charge. Lacking the foundries necessary to make a sufficient number of cannons, most were foreign purchases. (*US Army Center for Military History*)

(**Opposite, above**) To break the stalemate between the Continental Army besieging the British troops occupying Boston, Henry Knox suggested that cannons recently captured in upstate New York be brought to Boston to augment the existing inventory. Washington agreed, putting Knox in charge of task. It took six weeks to bring the cannons some 300 miles through to Boston, as pictured here. Once emplaced, they made the British occupation of the city untenable and ended the siege with a British evacuation. (*PICRYL*)

(**Opposite, below**) To provide enough firepower to Continental infantry formations, Washington and Knox decided to use small-caliber cannons brought in not by draft animals, but by manpower. These were referred to as 'battalion guns'. This illustration shows French infantrymen during a later European War. (*PICRYL*)

(**Above**) Re-enactors in Revolutionary War uniforms. For Washington and Knox, a major problem early on proved to be the lack of trained artillerymen. To fill that void, experienced French artillery officers were brought in (beginning in mid-1777) to train the Continental Army's artillerymen. Before that time, Knox had to depend on the limited experience of some American colonists and British literature on artillery employment. Knox himself was self-educated on the topic. (*PICRYL*)

(**Opposite, above**) An illustration of the Battle of Trenton, which took place on the night of December 25/26, 1776 and resulted in a resounding victory for the Continental Army. The Continentals, without being detected, managed to transport eighteen cannons over the Delaware River and into the town of Trenton, which was occupied by Hessian mercenaries. Once the battle started, Washington employed his cannons to quickly achieve fire superiority over the Germans, which the Hessians could not overcome. (*US Army Center for Military History*)

(**Opposite, below**) Portrayed here is the legendary Molly Pitcher, who supposedly took over from her husband in operating a cannon when he fell by the wayside during the Battle of Monmouth on June 28, 1778. Most historians consider Molly Pitcher a composite folk hero whose actions were based on the contributions made by two different women at different times. Wives served as camp followers and typically brought water to the front-line soldiers when engaged in battle. (*US Army Center for Military History*)

Following the end of the American Revolutionary War and as America began its west-ward expansion, it would encounter an endless succession of Native American tribes; an example of a Native American warrior is pictured here. Each tribe in turn offered varying degrees of resistance. Reflecting the typical hit-and-run fighting tactics of Native Americans, artillery proved of limited effectiveness. *(PICRYL)*

Despite construction of wooden forts along the westernmost frontier of the United States following the American Revolutionary War as shown here, tensions ran high between civilians and Native Americans. The artillery officer shown is standing alongside a cannon that would be considered garrison artillery as it is mounted on a naval-type carriage rather than a conventional carriage with a trail. (*US Army Center for Military History*)

In a very idealistic painting, we see Major General Andrew Jackson on the ramparts of his defensive earthworks that protected the city of New Orleans from assaulting British soldiers on January 8, 1814. Jackson based the strength of his defensive works heavily on artillery. The badly-implemented British attack resulted in an American victory, with around 2,000 British casualties and just 62 American casualties. (*PICRYL*)

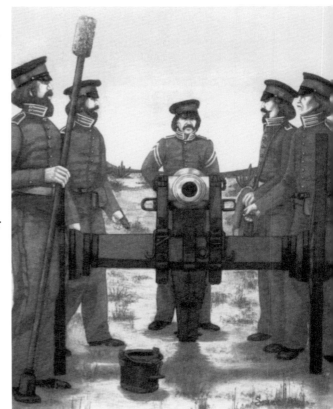

Using a translated French artillery manual from 1839 (adopted in 1841), the US Army's artillery branch reorganized itself all the way down to the individual cannon level. Gun crews were reduced from fourteen men down to just eight. The non-commissioned officer (NCO) in charge was referred to as the 'gunner' and was assisted by seven 'cannoneers'. It was the gunner's job to aim the piece and give the command to fire.
(*US Army Center for Military History*)

In the 1840s, America's civilian leadership was in an expansionary mood and set its sights on obtaining a disputed area claimed by the Mexican government. When US Army troops moved into the disputed area, Mexican Army troops attacked them, resulting in what became known in the United States as the Mexican-American War (1846–48). Depicted in the artwork is a US Army infantry officer in the foreground and an enlisted cavalryman during the conflict. (*US Army Center for Military History*)

(**Above**) On May 8, 1846, 1,500 US Army infantry, supported by three batteries of horse artillery, engaged a much larger formation of Mexican Army soldiers, also supported by artillery. The ensuing fighting became known as the Battle of Palo Alto, American artillerymen routed the opposing Mexican Army units. Pictured here is Major General Zachary Taylor ordering an artillery officer to fire more grapeshot at the enemy. (*PICRYL*)

(**Opposite, above**) On May 9, 1846 Major General Taylor again engaged the Mexican Army units he had defeated the day before. The resulting fighting came to be known as the Battle of Resaca de la Palma. Once again, American artillery took a heavy toll on the Mexican troops, allowing for American infantry and cavalry, as pictured here, to dominate the battlefield in another resounding victory. (*US Army Center for Military History*)

(**Opposite, below**) On March 9, 1847 a second American Army under the command of General Winfield Scott arrived on the eastern coast of Mexico by ship to mount an amphibious invasion of the well-defended port of Veracruz. US Navy warships added their firepower to Scott's own artillery, as pictured here, to breach the city's walls. The city's defenders surrendered after a twenty-day siege. Scott left a small garrison behind and headed towards the Mexican capital, Mexico City. (*PICRYL*)

(**Opposite, above**) On September 8, 1847, under a hail of American artillery fire, US troops under the command of General Winfield Scott assaulted the last major defensive position guarding Mexico City, Chapultepec Castle, as seen in this illustration. The defensive position fell the same day and the American general took official control of Mexico City on September 15, 1847. (*PICRYL*)

(**Above**) Portrayed in this illustration, US Army artillerymen (of different ranks) inspect a seacoast artillery battery sometime between 1851 and 1858. The US Army had undertaken a construction program of seacoast artillery positions beginning in 1816. Complementing construction were advancements, beginning in the 1840s (in the United States), in the design and building of large cast-iron cannons. (*US Army Center for Military History*)

(**Opposite, below**) Seacoast artillery carriages up to the early 1800s were made of wood, as seen in this photograph of a pre-war Columbiad cannon. The carriage pictured here is a modern reproduction. Subjected to the elements, the wooden carriages were not very durable without maintenance. They were supplemented by wrought-iron carriages beginning in 1819. Due to their low cost, however, large wooden carriages remained in use throughout the Civil War. (*Vladimir Yakubov*)

In 1811 there appeared the first American large cast-iron cannon, designed by US Army Colonel George Bomford. Subsequently, a whole line of larger examples entered service. However, they displayed a tendency to burst upon firing due to their brittle construction. Just before the American Civil War, Thomas J. Rodman, a US Army ordnance officer, developed a new method of construction which resolved that design problem. Pictured here is a 10in Columbiad built using the Rodman process. (PICRYL)

The shape and thickness of the barrel on the Columbiad cannons built using the Rodman process reflected the distribution of gas pressure generated when the propellant charge detonated. Obviously, the highest gas pressure existed at the rear of the barrel where the black powder and projectile lay prior to firing, leading to the old-fashioned soda-bottle shape as seen in this image of a 15in Columbiad/Rodman cannon. *(PICRYL)*

Chapter Two

The Civil War

On the morning of April 12, 1861, a 10in mortar round fired by Confederate militiamen exploded over Fort Sumter located on an island in Charleston Harbor, South Carolina. Confederate shore batteries bombarded the fort for thirty-four hours. As the fort was short of ammunition and supplies, the commander, US Army Major Robert Alexander, surrendered at 2.30pm on April 13, 1861 and evacuated the next day.

The Confederate seizure of Fort Sumter began the American Civil War, which lasted from 1861 to 1865 and resulted in the deaths of approximately 600,000 soldiers and 50,000 civilians. The US Army would, during the conflict, become known as the Union Army or the Federal Army.

Not Truly Ready

Neither the Union's nor the Confederacy's senior political or military leadership were truly ready for the conflict. The Confederacy was especially ill-prepared as it lacked the manpower, industrial infrastructure and other resources required to build weaponry (such as artillery) and furnish supplies (such as artillery ammunition) required by its armies.

Such was the shortage of artillery ammunition that Major E. Porter Alexander, chief of ordnance of the Confederate Army of Northern Virginia, wrote the following:

> The great majority of the batteries took to the field without ever having fired a round in practice ... The order 'save your ammunition' was reiterated on every battlefield, and many an awful pounding had to be borne in silence from the Yankee guns, while every shot was reserved for their infantry.

Only by 1864 did the Confederacy overcome its ammunition shortages.

The cannons and ammunition the Confederacy did manufacture often proved unreliable in service due to poor quality control. In a letter, Confederate Secretary of War Judah Benjamin complained to a Southern cannon foundry about their products:

> It is bad enough that our brave defenders should expose their lives to the fire of the enemy under such odds as exist against us, but to

furnish them arms more dangerous to themselves than to the enemy is utterly inexcusable.

To make up for its inability to build enough cannons, the Confederacy depended on other sources, such as captured Union Army artillery and cannons purchased from Great Britain. The Union, on the other hand, had the manpower and a sufficiently large industrial base to not only build new cannons in great numbers, but even replace all those lost in combat.

The Opposing Sides

Many of the senior officers of both sides had served as junior officers during the Mexican-American War; however, they were ill-prepared to command the ever-growing masses of poorly-trained troops.

Previously the US Army had consisted of only 16,000 officers and men divided among ten infantry regiments and four field artillery regiments. These were spread all over the country and received little training above the level of an infantry company or field artillery battery.

By the early summer of 1861, the Union Army had more than 300,000 men and the Confederate Army about 100,000 men. By war's end, about 2 million men had served in the Union Army, and less than half that number in the Confederate Army. (The lack of Confederate records makes it difficult to determine actual manpower.)

Trained artillerymen, both enlisted men and commissioned officers, were in short supply on both sides as they required more technical skill than the infantry or cavalry. The Union Army, however, had the advantage of a small artillery branch on which to build at the beginning of the conflict that the Confederate Army did not.

Artillery Batteries

By the end of the Civil War, the Union Army had formed 432 field artillery batteries. These each typically consisted of six cannons of the same caliber, though a few contained four guns and two howitzers. In the summer of 1864, Union Army field artillery batteries were each reduced to four cannons, all of the same caliber.

The Confederate Army formed 268 field artillery batteries, each with four cannons or less, consisting of both howitzers and guns, and often of different calibers and ranges. The diversity made it difficult for artillery officers to coordinate the fire of their field artillery pieces, as remarked upon by Confederate artillery officer E. Porter Alexander:

The variety of calibers comprised in the artillery was throughout the war a very great inconvenience ... At the commencement of the war, this variety was often ludicrously illustrated by single-batteries of four guns of four different calibers, and it was only after the battalions were well organized in the winter of 1862 that anything was done to simplify the matter.

New Tactics Needed

Both sides' senior military leadership had not yet appreciated the battlefield effectiveness of the latest weapon technology. One of these was the rifled musket, which fired elongated soft lead bullets known as the 'Minié ball' and referred to by American soldiers as the 'Minnie ball'.

The Minié bullet, incorrectly referred to as a ball, was invented in 1849 by two French Army officers and adopted by the US Army in 1855. It extended the lethality of small-arms fire up to 880 yards (0.5 mile). The previous generation of smoothbore muskets, firing round lead balls, was inaccurate at ranges much over 200 yards.

In the Line of Fire

Rifled muskets and their Minié ball made it impossible for field artillery to replicate the close-range tactics employed with such success by the US Army during the Mexican-American War, or by Frederick the Great and Napoleon. When a dire situation called for a field artillery battery to take up a position in front of their infantry – but in range of the enemy's rifled muskets – the results were often disastrous.

An example of this appears in a passage written by a Union officer:

> We were a considerable distance in front of our infantry, and of course, artillery could not live long under such a [rifled muskets'] fire as the enemy were putting through there. Our men went down in short order. The left gun fired 9 rounds. I fired 14 with mine ... Our section [two guns] went into action with 23 men and 1 officer. The only ones who came out sound were the lieutenant and myself. Every horse was killed, 7 of the men were killed outright, 16 wounded; the gun carriages were so cut with bullets as to be of no further service ... 27 balls passed through the lid of the limber chest ... The sponge bucket on my gun had 39 holes in it being perforated like a sieve.

Field Artillery Organizations

Other than the Battle of Palo Alto at the beginning of the Mexican-American War, the US Army had not massed its field artillery batteries to concentrate fire as had their European counterparts. As a result, as with the Mexican-American War, the opposing sides tended at the beginning to attach their field artillery batteries to individual infantry brigades.

The downside of keeping field artillery batteries at the infantry brigade level became quickly apparent to both sides, as was stated by Confederate General William Pendleton in 1862: '... this scattering of the [artillery] commands made it impossible ever to mass our guns in effective numbers. For artillery loses its effect if scattered.'

Eventually, both sides began attaching their field artillery batteries at the corps level. In the Union Army, five attached field artillery battalions constituted a field artillery brigade. Each artillery battalion, in turn, consisted of four or five artillery batteries. The Confederate Army did the same with its artillery battalions, which were the equivalent of a Union Army artillery brigade.

An 1859 US Army manual described the roles of the field artillery:

> ... to attack and defend the works of temporary fortifications; to destroy or demolish material obstacles and means of cover, and thus prepare the way for the success of other arms, to act upon the field of battle; to break an enemy's line or prevent him from forming; to crush his masses; to dismount his batteries; to follow and support in pursuit, and to cover and protect a retreat.

Both sides early on formed an artillery reserve in many of their armies. These were independent of the corps. During the Battle of Gettysburg in July 1863, the Union Army of the Potomac had sixty-seven field artillery batteries, twenty-one of which comprised the Army's artillery reserve.

The Union Army disbanded its artillery reserve forces in 1864 but re-formed them the following year. The Confederate Army of Northern Virginia had sixty-seven field artillery batteries at Gettysburg, with twenty-seven assigned to its artillery reserve.

The field artillery batteries (organized into brigades or battalions) of the artillery reserve were to be called upon by individual corps commanders, or the chief of artillery for the Army in question, to support or fill in gaps when the front-line divisional field artillery batteries could not. During the Battle of Gettysburg, the artillery reserve of the Army of the Potomac provided their ammunition to their front-line batteries.

The title of chief of artillery went to senior artillery officers on both sides during the American Civil War. They oversaw both front-line artillery units as well as the artillery reserve formations of individual armies.

The Effects of Massed Artillery Fire

An example of the effectiveness of massing artillery took place during the Battle of Malvern Hill on July 1, 1862. Colonel Henry J. Hunt (1819–89), a Union Army artillery officer, managed to assemble 60 of 250 artillery pieces to concentrate their fire. He then went on to destroy Confederate batteries one by one as each deployed on the field of battle. His massed artillery then repulsed three large Confederate Army infantry attacks, with minimum losses to the Union Army.

Colonel (later General) Hunt would bring his considerable skill in artillery tactics to other important battles of the Civil War, including Gettysburg. Upon the conclusion of the Battle of Gettysburg, a Union Army soldier inspecting the battlefield commented on the artillery's effect on the attacking Confederate infantry:

> Corpses strewed the ground at every step. Arms, heads, legs, and parts of dismembered bodies were scattered all about, and sticking among the roads and against the trunks of trees, hair, brains, entrails, and shreds of human flesh hung, a disgusting, sickening, heart-rending spectacle to our young minds. It was indeed a charnel-house, a butcher's pen, with man as the victim.

Pre-Civil War Cannons

At the beginning of the Civil War the US Army's primary cannons were the bronze, smoothbore, 6-pounder gun M1841 (3.67in bore) or the bronze, smoothbore 12-pounder howitzer (4.62in bore). The latter was also designated the Model 1841.

As both were considered obsolete as the war started, the Union Army quickly banished the 6-pounder gun to secondary theaters of combat and pulled the 12-pounder howitzer Model 1841 from service altogether.

Lacking sufficient cannons of all types, the Confederate Army retained the 6-pounder gun until 1863 and the 12-pounder howitzer Model 1841 throughout the conflict. In early 1842, a shortage of bronze resulted in bronze church bells across the Confederacy going off to foundries to be melted down and recast as cannons.

A senior Confederate Army artillery officer stated in an early 1864 report that the 12-pounder howitzer M1841 was 'scarcely more valuable' than the 6-pounder guns that he considered 'nearly useless, if not indeed worse'. To supplement the 12-pounder howitzer Model 1841, the Confederate Army fielded seventy-five units of the 12-pounder howitzer Model 1842, some constructed of cast-iron and some from bronze.

Mountain Howitzer

Another howitzer in limited use in secondary theaters by both sides was the bronze, smoothbore 12-pounder Model 1841 Mountain Howitzer (4.62in bore). Like the 6-pounder gun and the 12-pounder howitzer M1841, it dated from before the Mexican-American War.

With the 12-pounder Model 1841 Mountain Howitzer's barrel elevated at 5 degrees it had a maximum range of approximately 1,000 yards. The barrel and carriage weighed in at around 500lb and broke down into three components for transport by pack animals in situations where roads did not exist.

The Napoleon

In 1855, the War Department sent Captain Alfred Mordecai of the US Army Ordnance Department to Europe on a fact-finding tour that lasted until the following year. In his report, he mentioned that the French Army was in the process of adopting a new 12-pounder (4.62in bore) bronze cannon as its sole field artillery piece.

What made the new cannon's design special is that it successfully combined the attributes of both gun and howitzer. The nickname of the new gun/howitzer was the 'Napoleon'. That name did not refer to Napoleon Bonaparte, but Napoleon III, Napoleon Bonaparte's nephew and the last French king (1852–70).

Early Opinions

The Napoleon cannon impressed everybody who observed it, resulting in other armies quickly adopting it in the 1850s. Mordecai was a bit less impressed. He felt it was less durable than the existing US Army 12-pounder howitzer Model 1841. Others were not as concerned with that issue as Mordecai, and the new cannon proved in testing to be far superior to any of the existing US Army field artillery pieces.

The Napoleon's positive test results led the Secretary of War Jefferson Davis (1853–57), later President of the Confederacy, to announce in 1856 the weapon's adoption by the US Army as the 12-pounder gun M1857. In the process, it replaced the existing 6-pounder gun, the 12-pounder howitzer M1841 and the 12-pounder Mountain Howitzer Model 1861.

In 1857, American industry constructed its first Napoleon cannon. Yet it would not go into full-scale production until 1861 with the beginning of the Civil War. Including cannon and carriage, the Napoleon weighed 3,665lb and required a team of six horses. Its maximum range at an elevation of 5 degrees was around 1,700 yards. A well-trained crew could fire four rounds per minute.

To distinguish the 12-pounder Napoleon from the older-generation 12-pounder howitzer M1841, Civil War manuals listed the Napoleon as the 'light 12-pounder'. It was also officially labeled the 'Gun-Howitzer'. By the end of the Civil War, Union foundries had delivered 1,156 Napoleon cannons.

Into Combat

During the Civil War's opening months, a Union Army artillery officer spoke very highly of the new Napoleon cannons his unit received: 'Their firing is very accurate, and with equal mobility, they have much greater power than the 6-pounder. Each is perfectly adapted to the use of all the projects known in the service – shot, shell, spherical case, and canister.'

The table of fire in the Napoleon's manual specified the type of ammunition to use at different ranges. When firing on enemy forces under cover, natural or man-made, the manual stated that shell should be used up to 1,500 yards, not just for physical damage but to affect the enemy's morale.

The manual went on to state that the optimum range for shrapnel fired at troop formations lay between 500 and 1,500 yards, and canister at ranges under 500 yards. At ranges of 600 to 2,000 yards shot was suggested for firing at massed enemy troops.

What shot was capable of appears in a Union Army manual: 'The precise effects of a single ball cannot be accurately stated. Cases are sited where thirty to forty men have been disabled by a single shot, but it is laid down in principle that a 6- or 12-pound ball will go through six men at 800 yards' distance.'

Confederate Copies

Well aware of the superiority imparted to the Union Army by fielding a large number of Napoleon cannons, General Robert E. Lee wrote to the Confederate Secretary of War in December 1862, suggesting that if not enough bronze was available to build a sufficient number of Napoleon

---

Canister Impressions

For stopping large formations of attacking infantry, the Napoleon had no equal when firing canister. Union Army Brigadier General John Corse would state: 'No [infantry] column can stand a concentrated fire of six Napoleons by volley or battery ... [armed] with canister.' A Union Army officer present at the Battle of Gettysburg who observed the effects of canister fire on advancing Confederate infantrymen famously said that the enemy 'went down like grass before the scythe'.

A junior Union Army artillery officer would comment after a particularly hard-fought engagement: 'What saved me was that I had a whole lot of canister. When those rebels were charging us, we were sending 3,000 bullets a minute into them. Though everything was going to smash around us, my battery, somehow, kept in good shape, we lost only fourteen men.'

cannons for the Confederate Army that all bronze 6-pounder guns and bronze 12-pounder howitzer M1841s in inventory be melted down and recast as Napoleon cannons.

As with most copies of Union artillery, the Confederate foundries' versions lacked quality of construction compared to those built in Union foundries. A Confederate artilleryman made a comment on his battery receiving a Confederate copy of a Napoleon: 'We received our howitzers last night. They proved of a very inferior quality, especially the woodwork which is too weak to stand hard usage.'

In 1863, the Union Army seized the copper mines on which the Confederate foundries depended for constructing bronze Napoleon cannons. This forced the Confederate foundries to make all their Napoleon cannons out of thick cast-iron, which proved successful.

A Confederate artilleryman would comment on the cast-iron copy of the Napoleon: '... the iron gun was not only equally safe from explosion, but soon accomplished every purpose against the foe possible with the brass [bronze] gun and did not create the sharp, piercing ring so severe as not infrequently caused blood to break from the ear of the cannoneer.' By the time the Civil War ended, Confederate foundries had delivered a total of 501 Napoleon copies.

The Parrott Guns

A gun that appeared in US Army service just before the Civil War was named the 'Parrott' after its designer, Robert P. Parrott. He had started his

---

Recoil

None of the field artillery cannons employed by either side during the Civil War had a recoil system. Neither were they equipped with spades. Only by allowing their carriages to move rearward upon firing without hindrance could they absorb the massive recoil shock generated without serious damage. Following every round fired, cannon crews had to push their weapons back into their original firing positions, referred to as in battery, and re-sight them.

Samuel R. Watkins, a Confederate Army infantryman, commented on what he observed of a nearby cannon during an engagement: 'Here comes one piece of artillery from the Mississippi battery ... At every discharge, it would bounce, and turn its muzzle completely to the rear, when those ole [sic] artillery soldiers would return it to its place ...' Within the confines of wooden men-of-war, large, thick ropes absorbed and retarded recoil of onboard cannons.

career as a US Army officer but resigned in 1836 to run a commercial foundry.

Parrott's first gun design appeared in 1860. It was classified as a 10-pounder and came in two different sizes: one had a 2.9in bore and the other a 3in bore. Eventually, the Union Army discontinued production of the first in favor of producing the latter. All the 2.9in guns were eventually bored out to 3in.

At an elevation of 5 degrees, the 3in bore Parrott gun had a maximum range of just over 1 mile, and at 20 degrees elevation, a range of about 3 miles. The gun and carriage together weighed 890lb. The 20-pounder Parrott (3.67in bore) at an elevation of 5 degrees had a maximum range of just over 1 mile. The largest Parrott gun employed by the Union Army in the field artillery had a barrel that weighed 1,800lb.

The Larger Parrott Guns

Parrott's gun designs eventually encompassed an entire range of sizes, including shipboard, siege and seacoast artillery. In the siege artillery role, the Union Army used the Parrott 30-pounder. It weighed 6,500lb including barrel and carriage. Due to its weight and size, a ten-horse team was required to move it. At an elevation of 15 degrees, the 30-pounder Parrott gun could fire a projectile out to a range of almost 3 miles.

Parrott also built 100-, 200-, 300- and even a 600-pounder versions for the seacoast artillery and the naval roles. The 300-pounder had a 10in bore and, when elevated at 35 degrees, a maximum range of around 5 miles. The cannon barrel and carriage together weighed approximately 13 tons.

An article appearing in the August 12, 1863 edition of the *Washington Republican* newspaper described the power of one of Parrott's larger guns: 'The 10in rifle 300-pound shot has an initial velocity of 1,111 feet, and has afterward a remaining velocity of 700 feet per second, at a distance of 3,500 yards ... The penetration of the 10-inch projectile will, therefore, be between 6 and 7 feet into the same material [brick].'

Rifling

Parrott's gun series differed from earlier muzzle-loading, smoothbore guns and howitzers because they were rifled muzzle-loaders. Rifling refers to spiral grooves cut into the surface of the bore of a cannon that causes the projectile to rotate in flight. That rotary motion stabilizes the projectile, which in turn provides greater accuracy and longer range. Parrott's cannons used five rifling grooves, engaged by an expanding brass ring at each projectile's base.

Parrott Cannon Problems

Parrott's gun barrels were made of cast-iron, reinforced at the breech with wrought-iron hoops. Nevertheless, Parrott's guns (particularly the larger models with larger propellant charges) were known to burst when fired, an unnerving trait for the artillerymen who served the weapons. Union Army Private Augustus Buell would write, 'If anything could justify desertion by a cannoneer, it would be assignment to a Parrott battery.'

Despite this recurring problem, the Parrott guns were widely employed by both sides during the Civil War, both on land and on warships. Union Army Major General Quincy A. Gillmore was mindful of the Parrott gun's shortcomings but still stated that in the big picture of things 'There is perhaps, no better system of rifled cannon than Parrots [*sic*]; certainly none more simple in construction, more easily understood, or that can with more safety be placed in the hands of inexperienced men for use.'

Like so many other Union Army cannons, Confederate foundries copied Parrott's designs. Much to their dismay, their Parrott copies shared the same propensity as their Union Army counterparts to suffer breech explosions.

A Confederate artillery officer blamed his battery's failure during battle '... solely to the utter worthlessness of the 20-pounder Parrots, which had hung around our necks like a millstone during the march and failed us in the vital moment.' During the Battle of Fredericksburg (December 11–15, 1862), the Confederate Army of Northern Virginia employed two 30-pounder Parrott copies. The barrels on both burst before firing sixty rounds.

The weapon's inventor was very aware of the problems that plagued his cannon design. He would state: 'I do not profess to think that they are the best gun in the world, but I think they were the best practical thing that could be done at the time, and I suppose that was the reason for getting them ...'

James Rifle

Charles T. James (1805–62), an American engineer, Congressman and militia general, designed a new rifled, muzzle-loading bronze cannon classified as a 14-pounder (3.8in bore). It fired a series of specialized cast-iron projectiles, each of which was attached to a lead sabot. The weapon became the 'James rifle' and was only employed by the Union Army in the early part of the Civil War. The Confederate Army captured a few examples.

A number of the Union Army's older-generation cast-iron, smooth-bore muzzle-loaders were also rifled using James's system to fire larger versions of his cast-iron projectiles. As new rifled muzzle-loaders entered service with the Union Army, all the James rifles, as well as those smooth-bore cannons adapted for the James rifling system, found themselves pulled from service.

Not a Positive Experience

A couple of design issues dogged the James rifle. Bronze proved too soft a metal for cast-iron rifled projectiles, rendering the guns useless very quickly in the sustained fire role. His projectiles' lead sabots would fall off as the shells left the barrel, making them unsafe to fire over friendly personnel.

The first time artillery successfully fired over their own infantry occurred during the Siege of San Sebastian in 1813 in Spain, during the Peninsular Campaign of the Napoleonic Wars. It also occurred during the Civil War, but not without an element of danger to the infantrymen in front of the cannons. An example appears in this passage from a junior artillery officer who saw action during the Battle of Gettysburg:

> It's a terrible experience to support [artillery] batteries when located in their front ... I don't believe men ever suffered more in the same time than those who lay along the road in front of the cemetery on that memorable day ... If you laid down on the ground and put your fingers in your ears, you got, in addition to the crash in the air, the full effect of the earth's tremor and its additional force as a conductor.

Another problem with having artillery firing over friendly infantry formations was the issue of projectiles landing short or exploding prematurely. During the Battle of Gettysburg a senior Union Army officer threatened to shoot the offending artillery battery commanding officer whose cannon rounds were killing and wounding his men.

Wrought-Iron Rifled Gun

Adding to the advances in field artillery during the Civil War was the introduction of a very successful muzzle-loaded rifled gun made of wrought-iron and wrapped with bands of cast-iron for extra strengthening. Wrought-iron had twice the strength of cast-iron.

The inventor of this new rifled gun was John Griffen, manager of a commercial ironworks. He built his first example in 1854 and patented the design in 1855. An improved version appeared in December 1862.

US Army testing of the Griffen gun in 1856 quickly demonstrated that the gun was extremely reliable. The Ordnance Department ordered four additional examples in February 1861.

In July of 1861, the US Army ordered 300 additional Griffen guns, labeled the 3in ordnance rifle. It would become the replacement for the 10-pounder (3in bore) Parrott gun. By the end of the Civil War, the Union Army had ordered 1,100 units of the 3in ordnance rifle.

A Confederate Army artilleryman stated during the Battle of Atlanta on July 22, 1864 that 'The Yankee 3in rifle was a dead shot at any distance under a mile. They could hit the end of a flour barrel more often than miss unless the gunner got rattled.' The Confederate Army was so impressed with the weapon that they had copies made.

The weapon at an elevation of 5 degrees had a maximum range of a little over 1 mile. With an elevation of 20 degrees, the weapon had a range of over 2 miles. The chief of the Union Army Ordnance Department would state that 'The experience of wrought-iron field guns is most favorable to their endurance efficiency. They cost less than steel and stand all the charge we want to impose on them ...'

A Larger Rifled Gun

In addition to the 3in ordnance rifle, the Union Army fielded the Model 1861 4.5in siege rifle and Model 1862 4.62in siege rifle. Both were made of cast-iron with the former firing a 25.5lb round with a range of almost 2 miles when elevated at 10 degrees.

A Union artillery officer stated that Model 1861 4.5in siege rifles 'were of great use from their superior range and accuracy, in silencing troublesome field batteries and...could be moved with the reserve artillery without impeding the march of the army ...' Confederate foundries made copies of the rifled guns.

Armstrong Cannons

Out of desperation, the Confederacy bought some British-designed and built guns beginning in 1862. Some of these came from the foundries of William Armstrong (1810–1900), a British engineer and industrialist. They were rifled and constructed of wrought-iron. A novel design feature of the Armstrong guns was the fact that they were breech-loaders.

Durability problems with the Armstrongs' breech-loading mechanisms led to the firm discontinuing the design feature in early 1863. Armstrong guns that followed were all rifled muzzle-loaders. By the end of 1864, Armstrong had switched from wrought-iron to steel in building his guns.

Whitworth Cannons

The Confederacy also bought British-built guns designed by Joseph Whitworth (1803–87). Among them were a 12-pounder (2.75in bore), and a

> **Steel Cannons**
>
> The armies of both sides in the Civil War were well aware of the use of steel in the construction of some European cannons, including both the British developments by Joseph Whitworth and the German developments by Alfred Krupp. Up till the mid-1850s, the disadvantages of using steel in the construction of cannons were its high cost and poor reputation due to early steel cannon prototypes bursting when fired.
>
> Things began to change in 1855 when Englishman Henry Bessemer developed a process to make reasonable quality steel at an affordable cost. The first army to order steel cannons was the Prussian Army in 1858. Due to pre-Civil War funding shortfalls and wanting to stay with what was familiar, the Union Army did not embrace the concept of steel cannons during the Civil War.
>
> The next big step in steel production involved both German and French engineers in 1865. They came up with the Siemens-Martin process which, complementing the Bessemer process, produced a large amount of quality steel at reasonable cost. This was a manufacturing ability lacked by American industry until the 1880s. The US Army finally began testing steel cannons in 1887, with positive results. By 1890, the US Army had 100 steel cannons in service.

seacoast artillery piece labeled a 70-pounder (5in bore). Both were rifled breech-loaders.

Problems with the breech-loading mechanisms on the Whitworth guns resulted in turning them into muzzle-loading cannons by sealing their breech mechanisms. The guns themselves were built from steel made to very high tolerances, something not seen before on any cannon design.

The Whitworth 12-pounder had an unheard-of range of up to 5 miles or more, almost double that of its smoothbore muzzle-loading counterparts. The British cannons were also extremely accurate. A copy of the *Engineer* dated April 22, 1864 stated that '... at 1,600 yards the Whitworth gun [12-pounder] fired ten shots with a lateral deviation of only 5 inches.'

The Union Army received six examples of the 12-pounder cannon in 1861 but never employed them in combat. Charles Knap, a Northern foundry owner, testified before Congress in 1864 and stated: 'It is a perfect thing to show the state of the art, but for actual service, in my opinion, it is not worth carrying [the Whitworth 12-pounder] into the field ...'

E. Porter Alexander, a Confederate artillery officer, would comment that: 'Their breech-loading arrangements, however, often worked with difficulty and every one of six was at sometimes disabled by breaking some of its parts, but all were repaired again and kept in service. Like the Armstrong cannons, the later production examples of the Whitworth were rifled muzzle-loaders.'

Blakely Guns

A British Army officer, Alexander Blakely, designed and had built a series of cast-iron rifled guns strengthened by bands of wrought-iron or steel. Unlike the Armstrong and Whitworth rifled cannons, they were not breech-loaders. Unable to sell his products to the British Army or Navy as they had already decided on the Armstrong cannons, Blakely found the Confederacy a willing customer for his goods.

The Blakely guns were not without problems. Their wooden carriages proved unequal to the demands of hard service and often cracked. General Robert E. Lee commented on another problem with them:

> We shall be obliged to rely on imported ammunition for the Blakely guns, as its manufacture requires so much expense and time as to prevent its preparation at our arsenals and, in addition, it consumes so much lead that it is found impossible to supply it without interfering with other demands for that article.

Pros and Cons of Rifled Cannons

Both sides appreciated the greater accuracy and longer range of rifled guns during the Civil War in the field artillery role. However, the thick smoke generated by guns and howitzers using black powder or the density of the foliage on many battlefields often limited the supposed advantages of rifled guns. A senior Confederate artillery officer noted '. . . that long-range, random shelling is very far less effective than it is popularly supposed to be. . .except where it can enfilade lines.'

Observation of artillery projectile strikes became difficult during battle. Both sides preferred smoothbore guns as they had larger bores than their rifled cannon counterparts and therefore fired larger projectiles, especially canister. It was the increased killing power of smoothbore cannons firing canister at close ranges that kept them from being replaced during the Civil War. At the end of the conflict, the Union Army's inventory of artillery pieces was 50 percent smoothbore cannons, mostly Napoleons.

Heavy Artillery

With the beginning of the Civil War, the Confederate Army seized a great many pieces of 'heavy artillery' (which included siege and seacoast artillery) from Union Army defensive fortifications and arsenals. These included Columbiads and Rodmans.

Despite this loss of heavy artillery pieces, the Union Army remained relatively well-equipped with an inventory of 755 siege cannons and 1,810 seacoast cannons in June 1861. By June 1864, the Union Army inventory included 1,694 siege cannons and 3,053 seacoast cannons; both figures included mortars.

Still Useful as Siege Artillery

Obsolete at the start of the Civil War was the smoothbore, cast-iron 24-pounder gun Model 1819 (5.82in bore), of which approximately 1,000 existed. An improved version designated the Model M1839 gun would also fall into the obsolete category.

Despite their shortcomings (weight and range), both sides would push the Model 1818 and Model 1839 into front-line service early in the war as siege artillery. They were considered the heaviest artillery pieces (10,550lb) that could be transported in the field without undue difficulty, taking ten horses to move them.

Effectiveness in Battle

In contrast to the employment of rifled guns in the field artillery role where their effectiveness was mixed, in the role of siege artillery, when firing at fixed defensive works, be it brick or masonry, they far surpassed the effectiveness of their smoothbore counterparts.

At one siege, the Union Army chief engineer calculated that large smoothbore siege cannons firing round shot would only have been effective at less than 700 yards. He went on to state that '... good rifled guns, properly served, can breach [masonry forts] rapidly at 1,650 yards' distance.'

A Union Army general reported to his superiors that 'No work of stone or brick can resist the impact of rifled artillery of heavy caliber.' In response to the threat posed by rifled siege artillery, the engineers of both the Union and Confederate armies halted construction of multi-level brick and stone forts in favor of earthen coastal forts and batteries.

Rifled Rounds

Instead of the round cannonballs fired by smoothbore cannons, rifled cannons fired the same types of ammunition but in a variety of elongated shapes. Rather than the term 'cannonballs', inert solid shot fired from rifled cannons came to be known as 'bolts'.

As elongated projectiles expanded when the propelling charge went off in the cannon, they sealed in almost all the explosive force generated, meaning it took less than half as much gunpowder to fire an elongated projectile twice the distance compared to a round projectile of approximately the same weight. With the advent of projectiles that impacted an object point-first, be it natural or man-made, the impact-detonated fuze appeared.

As could be expected, elongated projectiles fired from rifled cannons suffered a great deal less air resistance than round projectiles fired from smoothbore cannons. In turn, they could be made heavier without increasing air resistance, which in turn meant that they offered more penetration. The downside proved to be the behavior of elongated shell projectiles digging themselves into soft sloping ground before exploding, thereby greatly reducing their effectiveness.

A Confederate artillery officer expressed some frustration with their rifled cannons in 1861 due to the poor quality of ammunition supplied: '. . . our rifle shot and shells tumble or fail to go point first, so they had no range at all and were worse than worthless . . .'

Major E. Porter Alexander would write: 'The difficulties which beset the rifled guns and their ammunition were, however, even greater than those under which the smoothbores suffered so long, and they were never so nearly solved.'

Mortars

The Union and Confederate armies both employed mortars in the siege and seacoast artillery roles, as well as on ships. The largest was the 13in mortar designated the Model 1861. It had a cast-iron tube, weighed 17,120lb and fired a 220lb round at an elevation of 45 degrees, with a range of around 2.5 miles.

To improve the mobility of one of its 13in mortars, during the Siege of Petersburg (June 1864 to April 1865) the Union Army mounted a single example onto a railroad flatcar for three months. It received the nickname 'The Dictator'. A Union Army officer commented on its recoil: 'The mortar fired with 14 pounds of powder recoiled less than 2 feet on the [railroad] car which moved 10 or 12 feet on the track.'

The smallest mortar in widespread use by the Union Army during the Civil War was the Model 1841 24in Coehorn with a bore of 5.82in. The bronze tube and wooden carriage together weighed just under 300lb, making it very mobile. It fired a 17lb round at an elevation of 45 degrees, with a maximum range out to 1,200 yards. Confederate foundries made a cast-iron copy of the Model 1841 24in Coehorn and the smaller 12-pounder Coehorn.

In an 1867 post-Civil War report titled *Siege Artillery in the Campaigns Against Richmond*, the author, a senior engineering officer, recalled a personal observation on the effectiveness of mortar fire:

> ... a Confederate soldier was blown entirely over his parapet [a protective feature for personnel and armament from frontal fire] by the explosion of one of our [mortar] shells, and his body lay, the clothing consumed by fire, beyond the reach of his friends, who were deterred from approaching by our sharpshooters. To thus deprive an opponent of the accustomed protection of the trenches is well calculated to shake his nerves preparatory to an assault ...

The Wiard Artillery Pieces

In 1863, the US Army Superintendent of Ordnance Stores, Norman Wiard, designed both a rifled gun and rifled howitzer. The former was classified as a 6-pounder and the latter as a 12-pounder.

Wiard employed something referred to as semi-steel in the construction of his cannons. It consisted of scrap steel mixed with both cast-iron and something labeled pig-iron. The mixture produced a product with high-tensile strength, allowing the cannons so constructed to have thinner barrels, therefore weighing less than their cast-iron or wrought-iron counterparts.

Wiard designed a new type of artillery carriage for his cannons that allowed for a much greater degree of elevation than the standard artillery carriages then in use. He also developed a new type of artillery carriage wheel featuring replaceable parts, which meant that an entire wheel did not have to be disposed of when damaged.

Despite Wiard's innovations in artillery design and positive comments by those who had a chance to employ them in combat, the Union Army only bought sixty-six examples.

Rockets

Somebody must have remembered the US Army's limited use of British-designed rockets during the Mexican-American War and wanted to see if they could still be useful during the Civil War. Unfortunately, the propelling charges of the surviving rockets had degraded to the point that most no longer worked. A few were, however, deemed serviceable and fired at Union troops on July 3, 1862. A Confederate Army officer present commented on what he saw:

> Their course was erratic; they went straight enough in their first flight, but after striking, the flight might be continued in any other course,

even directly back towards where it came from. Great consternation was occasioned among the camps of the enemy as these unearthly serpents went zigzagging among them … A few tents were fired, but the rockets proved to be of little practical value …

Eventually Confederate industry copied a new spin-stabilized rocket designed by British inventor William Hale (1797–1870). The rockets came in two sizes: a 2.5in-diameter version that weighed 6lb and had a range of up to 600 yards, and a larger 3.25in-diameter model that weighed 16lb and had a range of over 1 mile.

The rockets were fired from iron tubes mounted either on a wheeled carriage or on the ground. They would see some use by Confederate forces in Texas during 1863 and 1864. A single Union Army rocket battalion was also formed but never saw combat due to the extremely unreliable and inaccurate nature of their weapon.

In this illustration we see the opening act of the American Civil War as the siege artillery of the South Carolina militia (the Confederate Army did not yet exist) bombards the unfinished US Army's Fort Sumter, located near Charleston, South Carolina. The bombardment took place on April 12/13, 1861 and resulted in the quick surrender of the US Army command within the fort. (*Public domain*)

Both sides in the American Civil War anticipated a short conflict. Young men in gaudy uniforms such as the dress uniform of a Union Army artilleryman pictured here saw the conflict as a chance for adventure and excitement. Their respective generals, who had served in the Mexican-American War, lacked awareness of the technology revolution that had taken place with the introduction of longer-ranged rifled muskets capable of accurately engaging targets up to a distance of 300 yards. (*Public domain*)

(**Opposite, above**) Of the two sides' armies in the American Civil War, the Union Army had the advantages of numbers and industrial infrastructure. Artillerymen on both sides soon learned that they could no longer engage in point-blank fire with enemy infantry formations, as had the artillerymen of Fredrick the Great and Napoleon Bonaparte. Rather, they had to intersperse themselves among their own infantry formations to stay out of enemy rifled musket range and for protection. (*Public domain*)

(**Opposite, below**) Re-enactors fire a reproduction Civil War cannon during a public demonstration. The Confederate leadership, both political and military, must have been so convinced of a quick victory that it had obviously not considered the poor state of its own military readiness. Whereas Union Army artillery batteries typically had six cannons of the same caliber, the Confederate Army artillery batteries normally had four cannons or less, often of different calibers. (*Public domain*)

(**Above**) At the beginning of the American Civil War there remained a large number of howitzers in service with both sides. In this photograph is a Model 1841 12-pounder howitzer captured by Union Army troops. Pre-dating the Mexican-American War, it had the advantage of light weight (1,685lb) which included howitzer and carriage, but like all howitzers of the time its range of approximately 1,000 yards proved too short, restricting them primarily to a defensive role. (*Public domain*)

(**Above**) The most numerous cannon in use up until the beginning of the Civil War was the Model 1841 6-pounder gun, pictured here. Its main advantage proved to be its light weight (1,700lb, barrel and carriage together). Offsetting that design feature was the small round it fired that greatly limited its battlefield effectiveness. Quickly transferred to secondary theaters by the Union Army, the 6-pounder gun remained a front-line weapon with the Confederate Army until 1862. (*Public domain*)

(**Opposite, above**) The replacement for the Union Army's 12-pounder howitzer and the 6-pounder gun proved to be a French-designed and American-built cannon designated the Model 1857, pictured here. Reflecting its French origins, it acquired the nickname of the 'Napoleon'. Considered a gun/howitzer, the combination of barrel and carriage weighed in at 3,580lb. Maximum range came out at around 1,600 yards. (*Public domain*)

(**Opposite, below**) A wartime sketch of a horsed artillery battery going into action. The lifting handles on the top of the cannon's barrel identify it as the original production version of the Union Army Model 1857 Napoleon cannon. Subsequent models lacked the lifting handles. The Confederate Army would employ both captured examples of the Napoleon cannon and copies made by Southern foundries. (*Public domain*)

light 12 Pd ...

...tler's battery come into position.

ARW

A design feature common of almost all the Union Army's Napoleons proved was their barrels' flared front ends, as seen in this image. In military nomenclature the flared end of a cannon barrel is referred to as a 'muzzle swell', with the majority of Confederate copies lacking this design feature. As with most of the cannons built in Southern foundries, quality control proved poor, leading to less reliability. (*Public domain*)

A wartime sketch of a horse artillery team at full gallop. Union Army policy reserved the best horses for the cavalry, with the artillery getting the rejects. Horse teams had to be trained before going into the field. Of the two sides during the Civil War, the Union Army had an easier time acquiring the horses it required. The Confederate Army proved continuously short of horses for its artillery throughout the conflict. (*Public domain*)

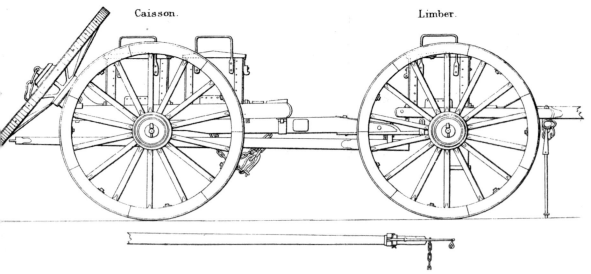

Caisson. Limber.

Each field artillery gun had two teams of six horses each, in theory. One team pulled the cannon and the limber, with a single removable ammunition chest, and the other pulled a limber attached to a caisson, as pictured here. The caisson had two removable ammunition chests. Typically, the rate of fire of most field artillery pieces during the Civil War averaged about one round per minute. (*Public domain*)

A rifled Parrot Gun pictured in a Civil War cemetery. One of the weapon's very discernible design features is the wrought-iron wedge-shaped bar wrapped around the rear of the barrel's breech, as is evident in this photograph. All the cannons designed by Parrot have this design feature, intended to strengthen the barrel where most needed. (*Public domain*)

PARROTT
10 LB. SHELL

(**Above**) A selection of cast-iron rounds fired from the rifled 10-pounder Parrot gun is seen in this photograph. A round fired from a smoothbore cannon such as the Napoleon was a 'shot'. When fired from a rifled cannon, such as a Parrot, it became a 'bolt'. While rounds fired from smoothbore cannons were all round, except for canister, those fired from rifled cannons were all elongated (bullet-shaped). (*Public domain*)

(**Opposite, above**) Visible here are four rifled 20-pounder Parrot guns. Even larger versions of the basic Parrot design were built for use during the Civil War. Parrot cannons were easy and cost-effective to build in large numbers by both the Union and Confederacy during the Civil War. However, they had a very poor reputation with most artillerymen, due to an inherent design flaw that sometimes led to catastrophic failures with barrels bursting upon firing. (*Public domain*)

(**Opposite, below**) Pictured here are a smoothbore Rodman cannon (with its classic soda-bottle shape) and a rifled Parrot cannon. There were no hydraulically- or spring-operated recoil systems available at the time. Upon firing, the barrel and upper carriage slid rear-ward up the slight upward track of the bottom carriage. The barrel's and upper carriage's weight and resulting friction aided in absorbing the recoil energy. The barrel and upper carriage were then pushed back into their firing position (in-battery) by the cannon's crew. (*Public domain*)

(**Above**) The artillerymen of a Union Army 32-pounder seacoast gun pose for this photograph, with the sword-carrying battery commander no doubt having inserted himself into the picture. The cannon's NCO, with the leather boots, stands on the right side of the image. Note the large wooden wheels, with metal rims, on either side of the cannon and carriage. These aided the artillerymen in moving the barrel and upper carriage back into battery. (*Public domain*)

(**Opposite, above**) Before the Civil War the US government had a number of large seacoast masonry and brick fortifications built to defend important seaports. What these lacked was a sufficient number of cannons to arm them, a process that took until the outbreak of the Civil War to resolve. The most common cannon installed in the seacoast forts were the 15in Rodman cannons as pictured here. There were also smaller models of the Rodman cannons, including 8in and 10in versions. (*Public domain*)

(**Opposite, below**) Next to the smoothbore Napoleon cannon, the most common artillery piece in the Union Army proved to be the 3in ordnance rifle pictured here. The wooden carriage is a reproduction. Built of wrought-iron, the cannon barrel and wooden carriage together weighed around 1,700lb. A total of 1,100 examples were supplied to the Union Army during the Civil War. Confederate foundries managed to build fewer than fifty crude copies. (*Public domain*)

(**Opposite, above**) Pictured here is a Union Army horse artillery battery, also referred to as a 'flying battery' as all the artillerymen are mounted on saddle horses. The men controlling the draft horse teams were not artillerymen and were referred to as drivers. The battery is armed with the 3in ordnance rifle. Maximum range of the weapon came out at approximately 4,000 yards. The cannon was well-known for its extreme accuracy at longer ranges. (*Public domain*)

(**Opposite, below**) In this illustration we see a horse artillery battery racing into action. Once the cannons were unlimbered from their horse teams, a wartime artillery manual stated: 'It [the battery] could come into action and fire one round in 26 seconds, timing from the order "action front" to the discharge of one piece.' Once unlimbered, the limbers themselves were placed 6 yards behind and facing their assigned artillery piece. The horse teams were to seek cover close by, if at all possible. (*Public domain*)

(**Above**) Canister was the most common close-range anti-personnel round for the artillerymen on both sides during the Civil War. A less commonly employed type of Civil War anti-personnel round, which pre-dated canister, bore the name 'grapeshot' with an example pictured here. It consisted of an arrangement of layered iron balls, with the number of balls varying by cannon size. Civil War soldiers often used the term canister interchangeably with grapeshot. (*Public domain*)

(**Opposite, above**) A Union Army heavy artillery battery armed with the smoothbore Model 1839/1845 24-pounder gun. The example in the foreground is mounted on a towable wooden carriage and the one behind it on a wooden barbette carriage. At approximately 10,000lb, including the barrel and carriage, the 24-pounder required a team of ten horses to move from location to location. The weapon's primary role was that of siege artillery. (*Public domain*)

(**Above**) To move large and extremely heavy seacoast artillery barrels (and mortars) from the foundries that constructed them to their final defensive locations required railroad cars and, for the last few miles, a specialized type of wooden carriage as pictured here. The barrels were slung under the carriages and pulled by draft animals to their assigned positions, where they were hoisted onto their pre-assembled wooden or metal cannon carriages. (*Public domain*)

(**Opposite, below**) Desperate for any cannons it could get its hands on during the war, the Confederacy turned to the British civilian arms industry for help. One type of cannon sold to the South proved to be the muzzle-loaded but rifled 150-pounderArmstrong gun pictured here. The large handspikes visible, used as levers, are for the gun crew to aid them in returning the weapon to battery upon firing. The biggest problem: the cost of the specially-made British ammunition. (*Public domain*)

(**Above**) Seen in this wartime photograph is a British-designed and built rifled Whitworth gun captured by Union Army troops. Unlike most other cannons employed during the Civil War, it had a breech-loading mechanism, which is visible in this image. However, the manufacturing technology to design and build reliable breech-loading mechanisms did not yet exist, and later production examples acquired by the Confederacy were muzzle-loaders. (*Public domain*)

(**Opposite, above**) America's pre-Civil War seacoast artillery fortifications (built of brick masonry) were intended to defeat Napoleonic-era smoothbore cannon fire. Rifled siege artillery introduced during the Civil War quickly demonstrated to both sides that they were obsolete, as appears in this picture of a badly-damaged brick fort. Post-Civil War, the forts were mostly abandoned and replaced by an arrangement of dispersed individual earthen barbette batteries. (*Public domain*)

(**Opposite, below**) Mortars in a variety of sizes turned out to be an important siege weapon during the Civil War for both sides. In this wartime illustration is an example of one of the smaller mortars employed during the conflict. It could be an 8in siege mortar Model 1841. Rather than battering down defensive fortifications, mortars were intended primarily as anti-personnel weapons, such as keeping enemy gun crews from manning their weapons. (*Public domain*)

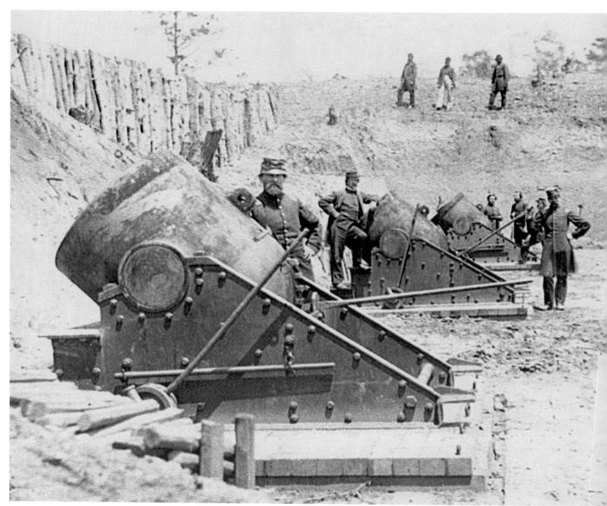

(**Above**) The largest mortar used during the Civil War by the Union Army (and Navy) was the 13in example pictured here, designated the Model 1841. It weighed in at around 17,500lb and fired a 220lb spherical shell out to a maximum range of 4,000 yards. Besides attacking enemy defensive fortifications, the 13in mortar could also be used to engage Confederate wooden warships as well as steam-engine-powered ironclads. (*Public domain*)

(**Opposite, above**) A very novel rifled cannon that appeared in Union Army service during the Civil War turned out to be the Wiard 6-pounder gun. The cannon's name came from its inventor, Norman Wiard, the superintendent of ordnance for the Union Army. He managed to design an artillery piece that proved to be extremely durable, with the added advantage of light weight. Despite glowing reviews by artillery officers, it was not widely adopted. (*Public domain*)

(**Opposite, below**) Invented by Dr Richard Gatling was the Gatling gun pictured here. The weapon would not be officially adopted by either side in the Civil War. The few that did see service were acquired privately and unfortunately proved unreliable in service. Though not considered an artillery piece, it was mounted on artillery-type carriages for mobility, thus its employment mirrored that of true artillery pieces. (*Public domain*)

Chapter Three

Into the First World War

Following the Civil War, there was a massive drawdown of the US Army's strength, including artillery. Foot artillerymen went back to manning sea-coast artillery batteries, labeled heavy batteries, with the surviving field artillery batteries classified as light batteries. The armament of the latter consisted of Civil War Napoleon cannons and rifled 3in ordnance guns.

It would take until 1879 before the US Army began testing a single example of a breech-loading cannon; in this case, a modified version of the rifled 3in ordnance gun. A second modified rifled 3in ordnance gun was procured in 1880. Successful testing led to an order for six more, with the last example acquired in 1882.

New Light Field Artillery Guns

The first new-built, rifled breech-loader for the US Army proved to be the 3.2in gun Model 1885. Made of steel, it fired a 13.5lb separate-loaded round, having a maximum range of almost 4 miles. It had taken American industry until the 1880s to produce quality steel at an affordable price.

Besides the 3.2in gun Model 1885, there were two other all-steel, breech-loading 3.2in field artillery guns built: Models 1890 and 1897, each a progressively improved version of the previous model. In total, the US Army acquired 375 units of the three different versions of the 3.2in guns between 1885 and 1899.

These 3.2in guns would see action during the Spanish-American War of 1898, the Philippine Insurrection (1899–1902) and with the multinational relief force sent to Peking, China in 1900 during the Boxer Rebellion (1899–1901).

Using Compressed Air

A most unusual artillery piece adopted by the US Army and US Navy in small numbers between the 1880s and 1890s was called the 'Dynamite Gun'. Rather than depending on gunpowder to propel projectiles from barrels at high velocities, it relied on compressed air to gently hurl dynamite-filled shells out to a reported maximum range of almost 3 miles.

The inventor was a civilian, D.M. Medford, who demonstrated a prototype in 1883, but the man who sold the concept to the American military was a US Army officer named Edmund Zalinski. The US Army saw it as a seacoast artillery weapon. Batteries of the Dynamite Guns went up on both the East and West Coasts of the United States.

There also appeared a field artillery version of the device referred to as the 2.5in Sims-Dudley Dynamite Gun in the late 1890s. Rather than compressed air, the field artillery version of the 2.5in Sims-Dudley Dynamite Gun used a small powder charge to generate the compressed air required to launch an 11.5lb round out to a reported distance of less than 1 mile.

Neither the coast artillery nor field artillery versions of the Dynamite Gun proved reliable in service and, compared to the latest generation of conventional artillery, lacked range and accuracy and were discarded by the US Army in 1904.

Next-Generation Gun

The US Army's 3.2in rifled guns had no recoil system to speak of, other than brakes on their wheels. To incorporate the latest trends in artillery design, the US Army began looking for a new field artillery piece. The result was the adoption of the 3in gun Model 1902. The US Army contracted to have 181 examples delivered between 1903 and 1912.

The 3in gun Model 1902 was a big step forward for the US Army artillery. In a March 1903 letter to the US Army chief of the artillery, Major William H. Coffin, President of the Field Artillery Board, Fort Riley, Kansas, stated: 'The passage from 3.2in field piece to the new [3in] rapid-fire field piece marks a new era for our field artillery.'

The 3in gun Model 1902 had a hydro spring-based recoil system. Also spades were attached to the carriage trail to aid in absorbing recoil. However, at the time of its introduction, the recoil system of the 3in gun Model 1902 was already dated.

Rapid fire became a capability of the 3in gun Model 1902 as its ammunition consisted of a metallic cartridge case attached (crimped) to the projectile, resulting in what was referred to as a 'fixed' round.

Ammunition Terminology

The metallic cartridge of a fixed round sealed the cannon's breech when fired and was semi-automatically extracted and ejected upon recoil. There are limits to the caliber of fixed rounds, as the larger the cannon, the heavier the round, making it impossible to load manually at a certain weight point.

A 'complete' round comprises all the components necessary to fire a weapon once. These components are, in general, the projectile, the fuze, the propelling charge and the primer.

The projectile portion of a cannon round is described in a US Army 1910 Coast Artillery Manual as the following: 'A term applied to a missile usually thrown from a firearm by some explosive, to strike and destroy some distant object. The principal parts of a modern projectile include the point or nose, the ogive, the bourrelet, the base, the rotating band, and the fuze hole.'

'Semi-fixed' rounds are supplied as complete rounds, as are fixed rounds. However, unlike the fixed rounds that have their metallic cartridge case crimped to the projectile, the metallic cartridge case of semi-fixed rounds is not crimped to their projectiles. Semi-fixed cartridge cases can therefore be removed from their projectile before firing to allow for adjustment of the propelling charge if required.

Rounds in which the various components – projectile, propelling charge and primer – are loaded into a cannon separately are referred to as 'separate-loading rounds' and are most common among cannons with a caliber of over 105mm.

Improving the Light Field Artillery Inventory

The US Army 3in gun Model 1902 would evolve through improved versions to the beginning of the First World War (1914–18). These would include the Model 1904 and Model 1905, with 40 of the former constructed and 441 of the latter completed by 1917.

The only conflict in which the US Army deployed any of the 3in guns took place during the Mexican Expedition (1916–17), during which time the US Army was supposed to capture the Mexican revolutionary known as Francisco 'Pancho' Villa. The army failed in its mission, and the field artillery batteries stationed along the American-Mexican border never fired a round in anger.

Training Issues

Having acquired more modern field artillery pieces was one thing for the US Army. Just as important would be the training required to operate artillery effectively. Prior to the First World War, that was a serious problem for the US Army.

The first commandant of the new School of Fire for Field Artillery, established at Fort Sill, Oklahoma in 1911, was Captain Dan T. Moore. He had observed the training conducted at the German Army artillery school before his appointment as the school's commandant.

What Moore saw with the first class of US Army artillerymen left him very concerned. He therefore wrote two letters to the US Army chief of artillery in January 1912, lamenting how far behind his students were in

Indirect Fire

The Russo-Japanese War (1904–1905) is the earliest conflict in which indirect fire occurred on a large scale, rather than direct fire. The reason was that direct-fire field artillery pieces were ever more susceptible to enemy counter-battery fire, as well as the ever-increasing range of the latest generation of small arms. This included the machine gun, with the first practical self-powered example having appeared in 1884.

Indirect fire had been employed on a limited basis for over 100 years, mostly in siege and seacoast artillery, by estimating the enemy's position, or by consulting range tables referred to as firing plots in the seacoast artillery. However, the slow rate of fire for cannons and their lack of recoil systems led to the opinion that it was of questionable value.

The only means of artillery communication before the field telephone were things like flag signals and the telegraph, which became practical in the mid-1800s. However, the advent of fast-firing guns with recoil systems, field telephones first used during the Second Boer War (1889–1902) and artillery forward observers (FOs) using maps led to more accurately-controlled indirect fire.

From the book titled *The Organizational History of Field Artillery (1775–2003)* is a summing-up of the use of artillery in the Russo-Japanese War:

> The effectiveness of artillery fire drove both sides to cover, that is, in defilade. Laying guns indirectly while in defilade became standard, with centralized control provided through the use of telephone wire. Indirect fire control resulted in an increase in the number of potential firing locations, and the ability to shift the fire of a great number of pieces without physically moving them permitted the use of heavier, less mobile artillery in the field.

By the time of the First World War, there were two different categories of indirect fire: observed and unobserved. The latter depended on maps, sometimes supplemented by aerial reconnaissance photographs, and practiced by the French Army. US Army Brigadier General Lesley J. McNair, the senior artillery officer in France, believed that the French Army's faith in the practice of unobserved indirect fire was a mistake. In a US Army publication titled *A History of the Field Artillery School* by Boyd L. Dastrup is a passage describing McNair's thoughts on unobserved indirect fire:

> A strong sponsor of observed indirect fire, McNair wrote that unobserved map firing was causing too few infantry casualties

> because it seldom engaged obstacles to the infantry advance as observed fire could. Whereas observed indirect fire offered flexibility, unobserved fire was rigid and prohibited adjusting to meet changing tactical requirements like observed fire could, making American technique superior.
>
> In spite of McNair's preference for observed indirect fire, it proved beyond the skillset of most US Army artillery officers in the last year of the war. This led to their penchant for employing unobserved indirect fire as there was more time to prepare for fire missions.

comparison to their German counterparts. In his first letter, he stated that it really made one shudder just how unprepared they were. In his second letter, he would comment as follows:

> I have never had such a hopeless feeling in my life as I had during the latter part of the last course [fall of 1911] when I found out that the student officers hadn't even grasped the elements and the firing they did was rotten. As a matter of fact, they did not seem to even grasp the rudiments, it was simply pitiful.

Moore's successor at the school acknowledged as time went on that incoming classes of artillerymen proved better prepared for the courses offered. However, in an annual report from 1916, he would comment that some of the better students still remained unable to conduct the more complicated task of indirect fire.

The School of Fire for Field Artillery was closed in 1916, but reopened in 1917 when America entered the First World War. It has remained to this day at Fort Sill and is known as the US Army Field Artillery School.

New Heavy Field Artillery Guns

To complement the 3.2in guns at longer ranges, the US Army acquired twenty-five units of the 3.6in gun Model 1891. It fired a 20lb separate-loaded round, having a maximum range of approximately 4 miles. During the Spanish-American War, some of them were placed into the role of seacoast artillery, with others slated for shipment to Cuba. In the end none saw combat, including during the First World War. Most were scrapped after the conflict, as were almost all the 3.2in guns.

The replacement for the 3.6in gun Model 1891 would be the 3.8in gun Model 1907. It fired a 30lb fixed round, with a maximum range of approximately 4.5 miles. The US Army only ordered eight examples of the weapon. They never went overseas and remained in the United States during the First World War as a training weapon, and were then scrapped.

The most numerous heavy field artillery gun adopted by the US Army before the First World War would be the 4.7in gun Model 1906. A total of 470 units came off the assembly line. Sixty-four went overseas with the American Expeditionary Force (AEF) to see combat during the First World War. Post-war, they all went into storage until finally withdrawn from the army's inventory in 1938. The weapon fired either a 60lb or 40lb fixed round, with a maximum range of approximately 5 miles for the latter.

New Heavy Howitzers

The counterpart to the 3.8in gun Model 1907 was the 3.8in howitzer Model 1908, of which the US Army acquired the first eight in 1909. After that was an improved model, the M1908M1, of which twenty came off the assembly line. Shell weight was 30lb, with a maximum range of 3.5 miles. Neither the M1908 nor the M1908AM1 saw action in the First World War and were used only for training in the United States.

The next step up from the 3.8in howitzer was the 4.7in howitzer M1907. It fired a 60lb semi-fixed round, with a maximum range of approximately 3 miles. Possibly through lack of funding, only four units were produced or procured. They were placed into storage and never used in training or combat.

As the replacement for the failed 4.7in howitzer M1907, there appeared the 4.7in howitzer Model 1908. By 1916, the US Army had acquired fifty-four units of the weapon. Fifty-five units of a slightly modified version came out of the factory between 1912 and 1916 and were assigned the designation 4.7in howitzer Model 1912. Neither howitzer saw combat and after serving as training aids in the United States and Hawaii were scrapped in the early 1920s.

Falling within the category of siege artillery when designed and built was the 6in howitzer Model 1908. A total of forty-two units entered US Army service between 1912 and 1913. It fired a 120lb semi-fixed round with a maximum range of about 4 miles. Like the two versions of the

Most of the US Army's pre-First World War guns and howitzers employed separate-loading ammunition and smoke-producing gunpowder. A few used a new smokeless powder, a European development invented by a Prussian Army officer in 1865. A French engineer developed a far more reliable form of smokeless powder in 1886.

Positive features of smokeless powder included increased range and penetration, as well as easier observation and not signaling one's position for enemy counter-battery fire. In a US Army manual dated 1910, smokeless powder is the name given to nitro-cellulose and nitroglycerin gunpowder. The first US Army field artillery piece that used smokeless powder was the 3in gun Model 1902.

4.7in howitzers, they never saw action but were employed for training in both the United States and Hawaii.

New Siege Guns

In the late 1880s, along with the introduction of the field artillery 3.2in, 3.6in and 3in guns, the US Army also took into service larger steel cannons. These included the 5in siege gun Models 1890 and 1898 as well as the 7in siege howitzer Models 1890 and 1898. The former fired a 45lb separate-loaded round and the latter a 105lb separate-loaded round, both rounds having a maximum range of about 4 miles.

Both the gun and the howitzer were pushed into the seacoast artillery role during the Spanish-American War, with some intended for shipment overseas. However, none saw action in the conflict. Some of the guns and howitzers were later shipped to the Philippines and others to Hawaii, but did not see action during the First World War. Almost all went to scrap dealers after the conflict.

New Siege Mortars

Complementing the new larger siege cannons introduced into US Army service in the 1890s were two new mortars: the 3.6in Model 1890, of which seventy-six examples appeared, and the 7in mortar Model 1892, of which sixty-one entered the US Army inventory. The only design innovation of the former was that it was a breech-loader. The latter would be technically interesting as it was rifled and had a spring-based recoil system.

The 3.6in mortar could fire a separate-loaded 20lb round, with a maximum range of around 2 miles. The 7in mortar fired a 125lb separate-loaded round, with a maximum range of approximately 3 miles.

Both mortars went to Cuba for possible use in the Spanish-American War, but never saw action. During the First World War, they were neither used for training nor sent off to see combat. Most ended up in scrap yards following the conflict.

Mountain/Pack Howitzers

Falling somewhere into the light artillery category were the so-called mountain guns/howitzers for use in minor conflicts, which the US Army considered between 1870 and the beginnings of the First World War. Small numbers of four commercially-available foreign-designed weapons were acquired. Three were foreign-built, with one built in an American-factory under license. They ranged in caliber from 42mm to 75mm.

Employment of the mountain guns/howitzers was limited to a few engagements with Native Americans between 1877 and 1887. By 1914, the concept of mountain cannon disappeared as there was no perceived requirement for such a weapon in the First World War. It was at this time that the term 'mountain' was no longer used, but instead the name 'pack' was implemented.

Some of the surviving mountain guns/howitzers saw combat during the Philippine Insurrection, with a few eventually transferred to the US Marine Corps. One of the four types, the 2.95in Vickers Mountain Gun, lasted in service long enough to be employed against the Japanese Army's invasion of the Philippines in late 1941 and early 1942.

Infantry Support Guns

Beginning in the late 1800s up until the First World War, the US Army looked at fielding smaller-caliber weapons, mounted on two-wheeled carriages, which ranged in caliber from 37mm to 57mm. The only example

---

US Navy Carriage-Mounted Cannons

During the American Civil War, the US Navy began acquiring landing guns (or boat howitzers). These were small-caliber cannons (no more than a 3in bore) mounted on two-wheeled carriages that would support landing detachments. The cannons had to be small and light enough to be manually lifted off a boat and also manhandled into action.

The US Navy would buy an entire series of progressively-improved versions of these from 1875 up through the First World War. As the weight of the last example acquired exceeded what sailors could lift in and out of boats, the weapons were given to the Marine Corps, which had been pushing the Navy for its own artillery pieces.

that proved successful was a copy of a French-designed 37mm gun, originally conceived by the French in 1885 and adopted in large numbers by the French Army in 1916 as the *Canon d'Infanterie de 37 Modèle 1916 TRP*. American factories would build 1,155 units for the US Army.

The American-built copy received the designation 37mm infantry gun Model 1916. Mounted on a small two-wheeled carriage, it could be pulled by a single horse or mule. When firing the weapon, it was detached from its carriage and mounted on a tripod. It fired a fixed round weighing about 1lb, with a maximum range of around 2 miles. The weapon's primary target was enemy machine-gun positions, although mortars eventually proved more useful in that role.

Besides those built in American factories, another 620 units were provided by the French Army. The US Marine Corps also adopted them. After seeing combat with the US Army in the First World War, the 37mm infantry gun Model 1916 remained in inventory long enough to see combat against the Japanese Army during the invasion of the Philippines in 1941/42. It did not remain in the US Army and Marine Corps inventory much past 1942.

Adopting the French 75

With America's official entry into the First World War (April 1917), the decision was made in early 1918 to adopt the French Army *Matériel de 75mm Modèle 1897*, best known to American troops as the 'French 75'.

The French 75 had an advanced hydro-pneumatic recoil system, the first field artillery piece so equipped and the standard up to modern times. It permitted the French 75's barrel to recoil and return to its in-battery position with the carriage remaining steady, allowing for the weapon's telescopic sight to remain on-target for successive rounds, not possible with guns that were displaced when firing.

The adoption of the French 75 was done not without some qualms as many in the US Army wanted to see the experimental American-designed 3in gun Model 1916 adopted into service. Unfortunately, testing that weapon in December 1917 the army discovered that it was inaccurate and that the two-wheeled carriage would not stand up under hard use.

French factories would build 2,800 units of the French 75 for the US Army, with around 1,800 entering service before the fighting ended. The remaining guns were completed after the war to meet contract obligations.

Rate of Fire

The hydro-pneumatic recoil system of the French 75, as well as a new fast-loading breech mechanism, allowed for an unheard-of rate of fire, easily up to twenty rounds per minute or more for a short time. A US Army report titled *Field Artillery Notes*, dated July 1917, states that a more typical rate of fire for the French 75 in battle was four rounds per minute and explains why:

> The reason for this comparative slowness is to be found in the fact that in some cases such fire must be kept up without stopping for four or five hours, and that there is a limit of physical endurance for gun detachments, and also in the fact that the experience of the war has shown that the life of guns can be greatly prolonged by moderation in rapidity of fire and care of material.

The French 75 fired a fixed round weighing around 20lb that had a maximum range of a little over 5 miles. It was also capable of indirect fire, using an attached rotatable, telescopic panoramic sight, a device that the US Army adopted for its 3in gun Model 1902. The German military invented the panoramic sight around 1890, which they referred to as a *Richtfläche* or lining-plane.

In American military service, the French 75 became the 75mm gun Model 1875 and was normally towed into action by a horse team. In the September–October 1918 issue of the *Field Artillery Journal* is the following passage: 'During the summer of 1918 the average life of an artillery horse at the front was set at ten days. Officers, fresh from training camp, were reminded forcibly of the obligation resting upon them for the care and conservation of horseflesh.'

American factories lacked the necessary manufacturing capability to build the French 75 quickly enough to see service in the First World War, with only seventy-four units finished before the war ended. None went overseas.

Post-war, American factories went on to construct more than 1,000 additional units of the French 75 for the US Army. The Marine Corps also adopted the weapon. Modernized versions of the French 75 would serve with the US Army until the beginning of the Second World War (1939–45).

More French Cannons

Despite many American field artillery officers going into the First World War with the belief that light field artillery pieces would dominate the conflict (as had the French Army in 1914), that proved not to be the case. Trench warfare, which began in 1916, dictated that the main reliance throughout the following years fell on heavy artillery.

The need for ever more heavy artillery pushed the US Army to adopt two existing French-designed and built cannons. These were the *Canon de*

155 C Modèle 1917 Schneider, a 155mm howitzer, and the *Canon de 155 Grande Puissance Filloux (GPF) Modèle 1917*, a 155mm gun.

There was a third cannon, a 240mm howitzer, based on a French design but it came off American production lines too late to see action during the First World War. In post-war US Army employment, the weapon, of which 330 were built, was designated the 240mm howitzer Model 1918. It fired a 345lb separate-loaded round to a maximum range of about 9 miles.

New Designations

In US Army service, the *Canon de 155 C Modèle 1917 Schneider* became the 155mm howitzer Model 1917, with a slightly different American-built copy designated the 155mm howitzer Model 1918. They fired a separate-loaded round weighing 95lb, with a maximum range of around 7 miles.

Only the French-built version would see combat with the US Army during the First World War. Between French and American production, a total of 3,008 units of the cannon came off the factory floor. From an article in the *Field Artillery Journal* dated October/December 1918 is an extract on the Schneider:

> Of all the varied artillery employed in this war, there is one gun of undoubted interest to the American artilleryman; and that is the famous French 155mm howitzer (Schneider). Its fame is justly won, for its long life, accuracy, and splendid recoil system have led to its complete adoption by the United States Army as the premier medium heavy howitzer.

The *Canon de 155 Grande Puissance Filloux (GPF) Modèle 1917*, in US Army service, received two different designations. The French-built model became the 155mm gun Model 1917, and the almost identical American-built model became the 155mm gun Model 1918.

Like its 155mm French howitzer counterpart, only the French-built version would see combat in the First World War with the US Army. The combined total of French- and American-built examples of the gun came to 997 units. They both fired a separate-loaded 95lb round, with a maximum range of around 10 miles.

All three of the French-designed cannons would remain in service with the American military until the Second World War. However, only the 155mm howitzer and the 155mm gun would see combat during the conflict, seeing service with both the US Army and the Marine Corps. The 240mm howitzer would remain in the US Army inventory through the Second World War but never saw action.

British Adopted Guns

The US Army adopted a modified version of a British-designed cannon built under contract by an American firm for use during the First World War. The British Army designated their cannon the 18-pounder (3.3in gun). The US Army version became the 75mm gun Model 1917.

Of the 909 units of the 75mm gun Model 1917 built for the US Army, most remained in the United States for training. The weapon fired a fixed round out to a range of around 5 miles. Some saw service post-war in both Hawaii and the Philippines. Those in the Philippines lasted long enough to see combat against the Japanese Army in late 1941 and early 1942.

A British-designed and built cannon ordered by the US Army for use during the First World War was the Vickers Mk XIX 6in gun. In total, the US Army ordered 100 examples and 50 spare barrels in 1917, although the order would not be completed until 1920. In American service it became the 6in gun Model 1917.

The US Army went on to also buy two different types of British-designed howitzers, which received the American designations of the 8in howitzer Model 1917 and the 9.2in howitzers Models 1917 and 1918. Of the former the US Army acquired 166 examples and of the latter 27 examples. Neither howitzer lasted in service long enough to see use by the US Army in the Second World War.

Guarding America's Shores

Following the American Civil War, General of the Army William T. Sherman and his successor Philip H. Sheridan both pushed for funding necessary to upgrade America's coastal fortifications. The advent of rifled siege artillery during the Civil War meant that all US coastal fortifications built before the conflict were now obsolete, making the country highly susceptible to attack by hostile foreign navies.

What the generals wanted to see were thick earthen defensive works (emplacements) armed with the most modern large breech-loading rifled guns. Influencing the US Army generals was the fact that Great Britain, France and Germany had already begun building a new generation of coastal fortifications. The civilian population of the United States also liked the idea as it seemed a more cost-effective measure than funding a large standing army.

Not Happy with Change

Surprisingly, up till the early 1870s, many US Army senior officers' preferred choice for seacoast artillery pieces remained muzzle-loaded, smoothbore cast-iron cannons. Besides their just not wanting to deal with new technology, they understood that American industry had not yet mastered the production of the high-quality steel required for building large rifled cannon barrels.

Congress's unhappiness with the US Army's preference for older-generation seacoast artillery pieces led to the formation of a special board in 1872. Its purpose: compare the latest artillery developments in Europe with the US Army's inventory. As a result, there was some thought given to having the army's muzzle-loading, cast-iron seacoast artillery pieces converted to breech-loaders, but nothing ever came of the idea.

Endicott Board

Congress had initially funded some minor construction work involving the country's coastal fortifications in the late 1860s, but that funding came to a halt in the mid-1870s. In 1885, President Grover Cleveland authorized the formation of a board under Secretary of War William C. Endicott to determine what was needed. The 'Endicott Board' recommended that funding for a total of 2,362 cannons be authorized.

When confronted by the Endicott Board with a price tag of $127 million, Congress balked and a much-reduced coastal fortification improvement program went into effect. By the time of the Spanish-American War, only 151 units of the newer seacoast artillery cannons and emplacements existed (typically open-topped with a surrounding wall of concrete protected by thick sloping earthworks).

Taft Board

In 1905, President Theodore Roosevelt formed a new board under Secretary of War William Howard Taft. Rather than acquiring and deploying a new generation of seacoast artillery pieces, the 'Taft Board', with a few exceptions, concentrated its efforts on updating infrastructure that supported the existing seacoast artillery guns. The Taft Board improvements included lighting, telephones and superior optical sighting systems.

Also, the Taft Board had new seacoast artillery defenses approved for construction in America's overseas possessions, such as Hawaii and the Philippines. The best example of that would be the construction of Fort Drum on a small island in Manila Harbor between 1909 and 1914. The primary armament of Fort Drum was four specially-designed 14in M1909 guns divided between two fully-enclosed armored turrets.

A New Artillery Branch

As the weapons and skillset required for field artillerymen and seacoast artillerymen began to diverge ever further, the senior leadership of the US Army decided in 1901 to divide the artillery branch into two sub-branches, field artillery and coast artillery, both under the command of the chief of artillery.

The field artillery included horse artillery, mountain artillery, siege artillery and machine-gun units. In 1907, Congress took the next step and split the field artillery and coast artillery into two separate branches, with the latter becoming the 'Coast Artillery Corps'.

Primary Armament

It took almost twenty years for the abridged Endicott Board program to be implemented and eventually resulted in the installation of approximately 300 seacoast cannons by 1905. The largest cannon was the 16in breech-loading rifle Model 1895. However, only a single example was constructed and not mounted on a coast artillery carriage until 1914, and then placed at a location near the Panama Canal.

The most powerful cannons originally intended for dealing with the enemy's capital warships were the 12in Model 1888, with progressively improved versions of the latter designated the Model 1895 and Model 1900. There was also the 10in Model 1888 and the improved Models 1895 and 1900. The smallest primary armament seacoast cannon was the 8in gun Model 1888.

The 12in gun fired a separate-loaded 1,046lb round, with a maximum range of about 10 miles. The 10in gun, with a maximum range of around 8 miles, fired a 617lb separate-loaded round. Unlike the 12in and 10in guns, the 8in gun fired a 316lb fixed round with a maximum range of about 7 miles.

The 14in Model 1907 eventually replaced the 12in gun as the largest and most powerful coast artillery gun. It fired a 2,100lb separate-loaded round, with a maximum range of almost 14 miles.

Seacoast Mortars

For the indirect fire role, the larger seacoast guns were supported by the 12in mortar Model 1886. It was made of cast-iron and was breech-loaded. The follow-on version, the 12in mortar Model 1890, was made of steel and also breech-loaded. It was considered a primary armament by the Coast Artillery Corps.

The 12in mortar fired a separate-loaded 1,046lb round, having a maximum range of 6 miles, with the high-angle plunging rounds intended to penetrate enemy warships' thinner armored superstructures and main decks. The thickest armor on capital ships was along the upper hull sides.

Twelve of the 12in mortars on fixed mounts would see action against the Japanese in the Philippines in late 1941 and early 1942. They were already considered obsolete at the time, and all those belonging to the Coast Artillery Corps went off to the scrap dealers following the war.

Secondary Armament

For non-armored or thinly-armored faster enemy warships, there was a variety of smaller-caliber seacoast artillery guns, including weapons ranging from 3in to 6in. First, there was the 6in rapid-fire gun Model 1897. Then an improved version designated the Model 1900, 1903 and 1905 was developed. These fired a 108lb fixed round, with a maximum range of 8 miles.

The rapid-fire 5in gun Model 1897, and an improved version designated the Model 1900, fired a 58lb fixed round with a maximum range of about 6 miles. A level below this was the American-designed and built 4in rapid-fire Driggs-Schroeder gun, which fired a 33lb fixed round with a maximum range of around 5 miles.

The fear of a Spanish fleet bombarding American cities pushed the US Army to buy two types of guns from British industry as a short-term fix. The 4.7in and 6in Armstrong guns were both of the most modern types and were referred to as quick-firing guns. The last of these foreign seacoast artillery guns remained in the army's inventory until 1927 before going to the scrap dealers.

3in and Smaller

The Driggs-Seabury firm supplied the army with the 3in (15-pounder) rapid-fire gun Model 1898, as well as a 2.24in rapid-fire (6-pounder) gun Model 1900 that when deployed in the seacoast artillery role remained on its two-wheeled carriage, which was then attached to a turntable to give it a wide arc of fire.

Disappearing Gun Carriages

Pre-First World War US Army seacoast artillery guns ranging from 6in to 14in bores were often mounted on disappearing gun carriages. A description of the gun carriage design appears in a 1910 US Army Manual as 'A gun carriage so constructed that it will carry its gun to a firing position above the parapet and upon discharge carry it back to the original loading position behind the parapet.'

A Scottish militia officer, Alexander Moncrieff, invented the initial disappearing gun carriage system in 1882, though his design proved unsuitable for large guns with a bore of over 7in. With the assistance of the British Elswick Ordnance Company, he modified his original design to handle British seacoast guns of up to 13.5in bore.

The Endicott Board adopted the disappearing gun carriage system in 1886. Two US Army Ordnance officers, Adelbert R. Buffington and William Crozier, improved upon the Moncrieff concept in 1893, allowing for guns with a bore of up to 16in to be mounted on a disappearing gun carriage.

A serious issue with the disappearing gun carriage system proved to be its high initial cost and necessary continued maintenance. More cost-effective was the much simpler and more affordable barbette system. In artillery terms, a barbette is a mound of earth or a platform, typically concrete, providing a shield over which guns can fire.

The value of the disappearing gun carriage came under question by the British military. During tests conducted in the 1890s, it was determined that naval warships were unable to engage individual coastal artillery pieces accurately. The British military therefore had most of their disappearing gun carriages scrapped before the First World War.

By the end of the First World War, the US Army considered disappearing gun carriages obsolete, with the last US Army gun on a disappearing gun carriage going into service in 1919. A number were retained by the US Army through the Second World War as they still retained some degree of potential effectiveness and there had been no funding to replace them during the interwar period.

The American Ordnance Company also supplied a 2.24in (6-pounder) rapid-fire gun. The Ordnance Department designed and had built the 3in (15-pounder) rapid-fire gun Model 1902. It fired a 15lb fixed round out to a maximum range of around 4.5 miles.

Repurposed Coast Artillery Cannons

The US Army did not have a sufficient number of heavy mobile artillery pieces to fight in France during the First World War. By 1917 there were no longer any concerns regarding German warships bombarding America's cities. Therefore, some of the Coast Artillery Corps' cannons were removed from their fixed mounts and mounted on towed wheeled carriages for use in France.

The Coast Artillery guns selected for conversion to towed pieces included 28 units of the 5in gun Model 1897 and 123 6in guns divided between two different models. Some of the towed 5in and 6in guns made it to France before the war ended, but none ever saw combat.

Upon their return to the United States after the First World War, the 5in guns Model 1897 along with their towed carriages were all scrapped. The two different models of towed 6in guns were reconfigured as Coast Artillery pieces once again, and survived in service through the Second World War.

The US Navy Contribution

To assist the US Army, the US Navy donated forty-six examples of its 6in guns in different lengths (calibers) from its inventory of spare barrels. The army also went ahead and bought thirty additional 6in US Navy gun barrels from a commercial firm that had recently acquired them in a surplus sale. In the end, only a single ex-US Navy 6in gun went onto a towed wheeled carriage. It never saw combat.

The largest gun intended for a towed carriage and service in France had the designation 7in 45-caliber gun Mark II. The gun was a naval design as there was a proposal put forward that a US Marine Corps division go to France during the First World War. The US Navy thought it might need its own towed artillery.

Due to the weight of the 7in 45-caliber gun Mk II, the US Navy designed an unpowered, towed tracked chassis for the weapon. Twenty went to the Marine Corps and eighteen to the US Army. None of them made it to France before the fighting had stopped. Eventually, all the tracked towed mounts except one went to the scrap yard. However, some of the barrels remained as Coast Artillery guns during the Second World War but never saw action.

Railroad Guns and Mortars

Before the First World War, the US Army saw no requirement for railroad-mounted guns or mortars. That view quickly changed with America's official entry into the conflict; the US Army quickly recognized its need for railroad artillery. As there was little time to design and build a new generation of specialized railroad guns and mortars, the US Army did what the French Army had done and began stripping some of its coastal defense emplacements for the needed weapons.

The US Army selected 8in guns, 10in guns and 12in guns as well as 12in mortars for mounting on specialized railroad cars. The US Navy supplied some surplus 7in guns, and an order for the Chilean Navy for 7in guns was impounded and turned over to the US Army. As events transpired, some of the weapons intended to become railroad guns were never completed as planned, while of those eventually built, none saw combat.

The US Navy's Big Railroad Gun

The largest American railroad guns that saw action in the First World War were five 14in 50-caliber battleship guns mounted on special railroad mounts. Operated by US Navy personnel, they were in action from September 6, 1918 until the armistice ended the fighting on November 11, 1918.

From a 1922 government publication titled *The US Railroad Batteries in France* is a description of their purpose: 'They were used for strategical purposes entirely and fired at ranges between 30,000 and 40,000 yards [17 to 22 miles]. Other artillery, of which there was a great quantity, could accomplish with less expenditure of ammunition and expense all the results that were desired at the shorter ranges.'

(**Opposite, above**) The first all-steel cannon made for the US Army was the 3.2in gun series, with an example pictured here. Some 100 examples of the rifled breech-loading gun came out of the foundries between 1885 and 1891. Upgraded versions received the designation Model 1890 and 1897. The cannon saw service in Cuba during the Spanish-American War (1898) and the Philippine Insurrection (1899–1902). (*Public domain*)

(**Opposite, below**) A short-lived concept that went into service with the US Army proved to be a 15in and a 2.5in dynamite gun. The former became a seacoast defense weapon and the latter a weapon for the field artillery. Both employed compressed air to propel dynamite bundles at the enemy. The larger of the two dynamite guns lasted in service from 1894 till 1904. The field artillery version saw service in the Spanish-American War but did not impress anybody, so most were scrapped by 1904. (*Public domain*)

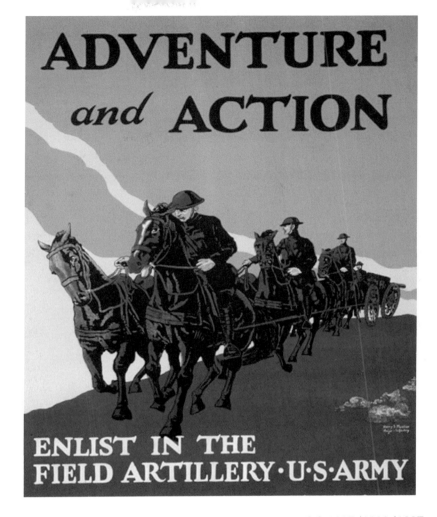

ADVENTURE and ACTION

ENLIST IN THE FIELD ARTILLERY · U·S·ARMY

(**Opposite, above**) Looking to replace the 3.2in gun Model 1885/1890/1897 series of guns, the US Army decided on the 3in field gun Model 1902. Improved versions led to the Models 1904 and 1905, with an example pictured here from the series. The problem proved to be finding a single American firm that could build the number requested in the required time. In the end, three organizations were required to complete the order for 662 cannons, including a German firm. (*Pierre-Oliver Buan*)

(**Above**) For many young men through the decades working menial jobs, recruitment posters like this drew them into army careers. The poster also highlights the fact that into the early 1900s, the army's field artillery depended on horse teams, as they had since the American Revolutionary War. The need to keep artillery pieces sufficiently light to be pulled by horse teams influenced their design parameters. (*Public domain*)

(**Opposite, below**) A picture of a Marine Corps 3in gun pulled by a four-wheel drive Jeffery Quad truck (prime mover), which first rolled off the factory floors in 1913. The vehicle saw widespread service during the First World War and proved both extremely durable and reliable. Insufficient funding during the interwar period prevented it and follow-on truck designs replacing most of the army's field artillery horse teams until the late 1930s. (*Public domain*)

(**Above**) Falling into the category of heavy artillery appeared the 4.7in gun Model 1906, with a total of 470 examples built by a variety of commercial firms and a government arsenal. Of those constructed, sixty-four went to France during the First World War to see combat with the US Army. It initially fired only a 60lb High-Explosive (HE) round, but to increase the cannon's range, a lighter HE round came into use later. (*Pierre-Oliver Buan*)

(**Opposite, above**) A short-lived howitzer in US Army service proved to be the 4.7in howitzer Model 1907. There must have been design issues as only five appeared. Its replacement, the 4.7in howitzer Model 1908, proved more successful, with 109 built. Unlike most cannons that had their recoil mechanism under the barrel, that of the Model M1907 lay over the barrel, enclosed by an armored shield as pictured here. (*National Archives*)

(**Opposite, below**) An old-fashioned concept that continued from the Civil War would be the US Army requirement for modern siege artillery. That need was filled before the First World War by a small number of mortars and cannons. One of these turned out to be the 7in siege howitzer Model 1890, followed by the upgraded Model 1898. An example of the howitzer series is pictured here. A total of seventy examples entered the army's inventory. (*National Archives*)

(**Opposite, above**) At the opposite end of the spectrum from the US Army's heavy or siege artillery, there appeared in US Army service a small lightweight (830lb) British-designed cannon referred to as the 2.95in Vickers Mountain Gun. A number are seen here in a Reserve Officers' Training Corps (ROTC) class conducted at an American college before the First World War. The army would acquire a total of 120 production examples. (*Public domain*)

(**Opposite, below**) Before the First World War, the US Army evaluated some weapons that fell into the light field artillery/infantry gun category. One of these proved to be the 1-pounder (37mm) Hotchkiss revolving cannon pictured here. It had five rotating rifled barrels that were manually rotated with a hand crank. Mounted on a two-wheel artillery-like carriage, the army bought nineteen examples, which saw limited use including during the Spanish-American War. (*Vladimir Yakubov*)

(**Above**) A strange and antiquated-looking gun which the US Army acquired to defend its seacoast fortifications against land attacks proved to be the 2.24in gun Models 1898 and 1900, with an example pictured here. It had a bore size of 57mm and fired a 6lb round out to a maximum range of 6,241 yards. The army eventually purchased ninety-four examples. None ever saw combat, and most were scrapped after the First World War. (*Richard and Barb Eshleman*)

(**Above**) Pictured here is an example of the 1-pounder Vickers-Maxim automatic gun on a vessel. The US Army would eventually acquire twenty-one examples of the weapon between 1900 and 1905. It would prove to be the army's first actual machine gun, although it fired 37mm rounds rather than bullets. On its artillery-like carriage it weighed 410lb, which made it unpopular with the army. It saw some service in the Philippines but not in the First World War. All left service by 1919. (*Public domain*)

(**Opposite, above**) A cannon adopted by the French Army on the outbreak of the First World War bore the designation *Canon d'Infanterie de 37 Modèle 1916 TRP*. Weighing in at only 109lb on its lightweight metal tripod carriage, it was used by the French Army to engage enemy machine-gun emplacements and strongpoints. The weapon pictured here was taken into US Army service beginning in June 1918 and assigned the designation 37mm infantry gun Model 1916. (*National Archives*)

(**Opposite, below**) The French Army adopted in 1916 a 37mm gun designed and built by the American firm of Bethlehem Steel. The company labeled it as the 1-pounder 37mm semi-automatic gun, Mark C, an example is pictured here. The weapon did not impress the French Army, which preferred their own *Canon d'Infanterie de 37 Modèle 1916 TRP*. (*Richard and Barb Eshleman*)

A 37

(**Above**) The most numerous cannon in service with the US Army during the First World War proved to be the French-designed and built *Matériel de 75mm Modèle 1897*, best known to American troops as the 'French 75'. Its official US Army designation proved to be the 75mm gun Model 1897. American-built copies of the French 75 did not reach France in time to see combat. (*Pierre-Olivier Buan*)

(**Opposite, above**) The French 75 proved to be the first field artillery piece with a modern recoil system that, with a well-trained crew, gave it a rate of fire of more than twenty rounds per minute for a brief amount of time. The pile of spent cartridges cases in the foreground attests to the number of rounds which the US Army crew fired in battle. The gun remained in US Army service until the Second World War. (*Public domain*)

(**Opposite, below**) Lacking any modern heavy field artillery pieces of its own and with American industry unable to design and build such weapons, the US Army again acquired a French weapon, the *Canon de 155 C Modèle 1917 Schneider*, the 155mm howitzer pictured here. In US Army service, it received the designation 155mm howitzer Models 1917 and 1918. Like the French 75, the 155mm howitzer remained in service with the US Army until the Second World War. (*National Archives*)

(**Opposite, above**) Another heavy artillery piece designed and built by French industry and taken into American service in the First World War was the *Canon de 155 Grande Puissance Filloux (GPF) Modèle 1917* 155mm gun. Only French-built examples saw combat with the US Army in France, with an example pictured here. These, like other French-designed cannons, remained in service with the US Army into the Second World War. (*Pierre-Olivier Buan*)

(**Opposite, below**) Other than railroad guns, the largest cannon envisioned to enter service with the US in the First World received the designation 240mm howitzer Model 1918, with an example pictured here. Its design, based on a successful French Army 280mm howitzer, was modified to meet US Army requirements. American industry was to manufacture them for the US Army's use during the First World War, but production delays meant the 330 units did not enter service until after the conflict. (*Public domain*)

(**Above**) To equip its artillery batteries with sufficient artillery pieces for the First World War, the US Army looked at all its options. An American firm had been contracted by the British government to build the 18-pounder (3.3in) gun for British use. The US Army arranged for the same company to build 909 examples of a modified version that became the 75mm gun Model 1917. Pictured here is the original British Army version in New Zealand Army service. (*Public domain*)

A British-designed and built cannon employed by the US Army during the First World War received the American designation of the 6in gun Model 1917. Some 100 along with 50 spare barrels were ordered in 1917, although deliveries did not end until 1920. With the outbreak of the Second World War, ninety-nine examples went to Brazil as military aid. An example is seen here in Brazil as a monument. The pneumatic tires were a last-minute addition by the US Army before they were shipped to Brazil. (*Public domain*)

The US Army desired during the First World War to put into service the 240mm howitzer Model 1918. It quickly became apparent that it would not be ready in time. As an interim measure, the US Army adopted a large British-designed cannon which it designated the 9.2in howitzer Model 1917 and 1918, with an example pictured here. The army acquired forty-four examples, which were disposed of by 1926. (*Public domain*)

Pictured here in 1918 is the US Army's most illustrious artilleryman, US Army Captain Harry S. Truman. At the time he was commander of Battery D, 129th Artillery Regiment of the 35th Infantry Division. Post-war, he rose to the rank of colonel and assumed command of the 379th Artillery Regiment of the 102nd Infantry Division. He is best-known as the 33rd President of the United States (1945–53). (*Public domain*)

The US Army Coast Artillery Corps came into being in 1917, split off from the US Army Field Artillery branch. The Coast Artillery School was established at Fort Monroe, Virginia. Pictured at the Sandy Hook Proving Ground in New Jersey are three coast artillery guns on barbette test carriages. From left to right are 8in, 10in and 12in guns. The largest of the three had a maximum range of 18,400 yards (10 miles). (*Public domain*)

From 1890 untill 1917, the disappearing carriage pictured here was the US Army Coast Artillery Corps' preference for its 6in and larger cannons. Invented by the British and much improved by the US military, it was described in a coast artillery manual as 'a gun carriage so constructed that it will carry its gun to firing position above the parapet and upon discharge carry it back to the original loading position.' (*Public domain*)

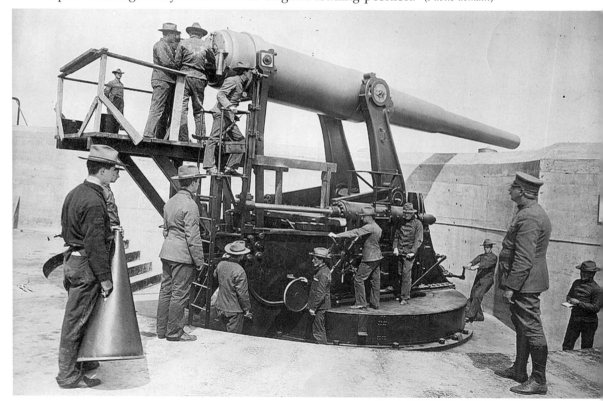

In this photograph, we see a 12in gun on a disappearing gun carriage in its fully retracted position. Typically, such a battery consisted of two separate guns of the same caliber, grouped with the object of concentrating their fire on a single naval target and under the command of a single individual. Very rarely would there be a single large disappearing gun carriage and the necessary fire-control equipment. (*Public domain*)

Loading and firing of large coast artillery guns depended on a great many men, as is evident in this photograph. The enlisted men serving the piece, labeled the 'gun section', were overseen by a specially-qualified non-commissioned officer (NCO) referred to as the 'gun commander'. He worked in conjunction with the 'gun pointer', who was charged with proper aiming or laying of a gun. (*Public domain*)

(**Above**) The crew of this US Army Coast Artillery 12in gun is using a rammer to properly seat a projectile in the weapon's breech. Once the projectile is in its proper position, silk-encased propellant charges were loaded into the gun's powder chamber, located behind the projectile. The cannoneers then close the breechblock. For larger coast artillery guns, the breechblock was of the interrupted step-thread design. (*Public domain*)

(**Opposite, above**) Among the array of weapons which the US Army Coast Artillery Corps acquired was the breech-loaded 12in mortar, a preserved example of which is pictured here. It came in three progressively improved models: the 1886, the 1900 and the 1912. American industry built 476 examples of the almost 80-ton (160,000lb) mortar. At an angle of 45 degrees, it could lob an armor-piercing (AP) projectile weighing almost 800lb onto the thinly-armored decks of enemy warships to a maximum range of almost 12,000 yards (7 miles). (*Author's collection*)

(**Opposite, below**) The original plans for emplacement of the 12inch mortars called for four to be located in small concrete pits (surrounded by high earthen embankments). Note that one of the mortar carriages in this photograph lacks a barrel. Rounds were transported to the breech-loaded weapon on carts (seen in the image). Eventually the army reduced the number of mortars in each battery to only two per pit to minimize the blast effect on their crews in an enclosed space. (*Public domain*)

(**Above**) This fanciful magazine illustration shows what an artist believed the 12in mortars defending New York Harbor would look like when all firing at the same time. The US Army initially did think to fire all its 12in mortars (at a coast artillery site) at one time, theoretically increasing the odds of actually hitting an enemy vessel. Eventually, as fire-control techniques improved, the army decided that a single 12in mortar could successfully engage and sink a single enemy ship. (*Public domain*)

(**Opposite, above**) Besides the massive guns and mortars intended to engage enemy battleships and cruisers at extended ranges of over 5 miles, the US Army fielded a large number of smaller-caliber guns. The example pictured here, labeled the 3in (15-pounder) rapid-fire gun, was fitted to a pedestal mount. These guns' targets were torpedo boats and mine-sweepers at close range. (*Public domain*)

(**Opposite, below**) From a US Army Coast Artillery Corps manual is another picture of a 3in (15-pounder) rapid-fire gun, with its various components listed. The gun had open sights to enable the weapon's gunner to quickly bring an object into its telescopic sight's field of view. Unlike their larger coast artillery counterparts that used separate-loaded ammunition, the rapid-fire guns employed fixed rounds. (*National Archives*)

Gun Shield

Sight

Front Sight

Cradle

Jacket

Extractor Hinge Pin

FIRING BATTERY

Shoulder Rest

Gunners Shield

Block Carrier Hinge Pin

Breechblock Carrier

Firing Mechanism

Tool Box

Elevating Handwheel

Traversing Worm Rack

Training Worm

Recoil Cylinder

Latch

Operating Lever

Sub Caliber Tube

Pistol Grip

Pivot Yoke

Traversing Hand Wheel

Pedestal

Foundation Bolts

1. 1-pounder.   2. 2½-pounder.   3. 3-pounder.   4. 6-pounder.   5. 9-pounder.
6. 33-pounder 4-inch gun.

FIXED AMMUNITION FOR RAPID-FIRE GUNS.

An illustration of the many types of fixed rounds fired by the rapid-fire guns defending America's shores, prior and during the First World War. A Coast Artillery Corps manual describes a rapid-fire gun as the following: 'A single-barrel breech-loading gun provided with breech mechanism, mounting and facilities for loading, aiming and firing with great rapidity. The breech mechanism is operated by a single motion of the handle or lever.' (*National Archives*)

ARC AND
OBTURATOR

GLASS
FRONT DOOR

DRUM

REFLECTOR
(MIRROR)

TRUNNION

STANDARDS

LAMP CASE

TRAINING
CLUTCH

ELEVATING
RACK

TURNTABLE

PEDESTAL AND
AINING MECHANISM

IOX AND
SORIES

AYS

LAMP

NEGATIVE CARBON

POSITIVE CARBON

RHEOSTAT

OLLER CABLE

POWER CABLE

To assist the rapid-fire guns in acquiring naval targets at night, the US Army added searchlights to its coastal defenses. There were two types placed into service: a 36in version pictured here and a larger 60in model, both with a maximum range of around 8,000 yards (4.5 miles) on a clear night. An army manual states that the best location for a searchlight was less than 150 yards from the nearest gun battery or optical position-finder. (*Public domain*)

Lowering 14-Inch, 50 caliber Gun into the Slide of the first Mount.

(**Opposite, above**) Lacking a sufficient number of heavy guns to supply the US Army infantry divisions being sent to France beginning in 1917, the army decided to convert some of its fixed coast artillery guns into towed artillery pieces. An example of that repurposing is the 6in gun Model 1900A2 pictured in the foreground, mounting the weapon on a wheeled carriage labeled the Model 1917A. The gun and carriage together weighed almost 40,000lb (20 tons). (*Public domain*)

(**Opposite, below**) Undergoing restoration is the only preserved example of the 7in gun Mark II, fitted onto the tractor mount Mark V. Twenty examples of the naval gun on its tracked carriage came off the arsenal floor for use by the US Marine Corps during the First World War. Firing a separate loading shell that weighed around 152lb, the gun had a maximum range of 24,000 yards (almost 12 miles). None made it to France before the fighting ended. (*Public domain*)

(**Above**) To offset the German Army's advantage of longer-range heavy artillery during the First World War, the US Navy offered five of its surplus 14in naval guns to be fitted on specialized railroad carriages, with the first example pictured here. They were to be disassembled for transport to France by ship and reassembled before going into action. The first US Navy railroad gun arrived in France on July 8, 1918. (*US Navy Historical Center*)

(**Above**) The five US Navy railroad guns, with an example pictured here, were in action for only the last twenty-five days of the war. They fired a total of 782 rounds during their time in combat. US Army General John J. Pershing said of the guns, 'our large-caliber guns had advanced and were skillfully brought into position to fire upon the important lanes. We had cut the enemy's main line of communications and nothing but surrender or an armistice could save him from the batteries.' (*Public domain*)

(**Opposite, above**) Having no railroad guns to send to France during the First World War, the US Army decided to have some of its Coast Artillery Corps' weapons re-purposed as railroad artillery. These would include 129 10in guns, 45 12in guns and 120 12in mortars, with an example pictured here. Few made it to France before the fighting stopped. (*Public domain*)

(**Opposite, below**) From an October 1944 US Army Coast Artillery manual is a passage on the advantages offered by railway cannons: 'Its tactical importance is paramount because its presence, even though known by the enemy, cannot be accurately ascertained since we possess numerous concealed positions to which railway mounts may be moved when deemed necessary.' (*National Archives*)

Chapter Four

Into the Second World War

Troubled about the need to depend on foreign artillery pieces in the First World War, the US Army formed the Westervelt Board in December 1918. (The board was named after its senior ranking officer, Brigadier General William I. Westervelt.) It was also referred to at times as the Caliber Board. Composed of seven senior officers, the board was tasked with determining the US Army's future artillery needs.

The board developed a wish list of ideal artillery pieces that would satisfy the army's future requirements. These would include four categories: light, medium, heavy and super-heavy. Their thought was that guns and howitzers of the same caliber could be fitted on identical carriages for the cost savings. Unfortunately, most of the recommendations made by the board in 1919 did not take place until the late 1930s due to a severe reduction in artillery development funding after 1921.

Towed 75mm Pack Howitzer

One of the few Westervelt Board recommendations to be put into place fairly quickly was the new lightweight towed 75mm howitzer that entered service in 1927 as the 75mm Howitzer Pack M1. The US Army's chief of artillery was so pleased with the howitzer that he stated in a 1932 magazine article: 'It is a remarkable weapon with a great future.' Despite the high praise, only thirty-two examples of a slightly improved version, the M1A1, had been built by the end of June 1940.

The original version of the 75mm Howitzer Pack M1A1 rode on a two-wheeled towed carriage fitted with steel-rimmed wooden wheels. As the US Army began considering the formation of airborne divisions (starting in May 1939), it decided that the 75mm Howitzer M1A1 would arm the cannon companies of their glider battalions. That called for the design and construction of a new all-steel carriage riding on pneumatic tires.

With Congressional funding becoming more generous in response to German military success in the invasions of Poland, the Netherlands, Belgium and France, the US Army stepped up production of the 75mm Howitzer Pack M1A1, on its all-steel carriage, in December 1940. By December 1944, when production concluded, American industry had constructed a total of 4,939 examples of the Pack Howitzer M1.

The Marine Corps took the Pack Howitzer M1 into service beginning in 1939. The weapon fired a semi-fixed round weighing around 15lb with a maximum range of around 5 miles. In the jungle fighting that sometimes took place in the Pacific, it proved its worth as it could go into firing positions that the larger and heavier 105mm Howitzer M2A1 could not.

In the April 1945 issue of the *Field Artillery Journal*, a Marine officer in command of a battery of 75mm howitzers on Guam commented on one of the hazards faced by all artillerymen through the ages: 'After ten days, the men were so deaf from concussion they had to stand facing each other and shout when they talked.'

Self-Propelled 75mm Howitzers

An early attempt to provide a self-propelled chassis for the 75mm Pack Howitzer M1A1 resulted in the T30 75mm Howitzer Motor Carriage (HMC). It consisted of a modified M3 armored half-track armed with the 75mm howitzer in a forward-firing position with limited traverse. Protection for the cannon crew came from an armored shield. The T30 HMCs would see service with the US Army in both the North African and Sicilian campaigns.

The T30 HMC was only a temporary solution. Work on a full-tracked carriage based on the M5 light tank series began in December 1941. The 75mm howitzer was placed in an open-top turret and serviced by two men. Successful testing of the T47 prototype vehicle resulted in production approval in May 1942. The building of what became the M8 75mm HMC began in September 1942 and concluded in January 1944, with a total of 1,778 built.

A Growing Need

The need for a new American towed 105mm light divisional howitzer was one of great controversy during most of its developmental history. During the First World War, US Army Colonel Charles P. Summerall visited

---

Interwar Odds and Ends

Besides the 75mm Howitzer Pack M1, the US Army also had a few experimental cannons it pursued in the 1920s. These included the 75mm Gun Model 1920, of which only four appeared. There were also twelve examples of a weapon designated the 37mm Infantry Gun M2, and sixteen of what became the 75mm Infantry Mortar M2. For a variety of reasons, besides the lack of funding, none were standardized (ordered into series production).

France on a fact-finding mission to observe new trends in artillery employment.

Summerall (later chief of staff of the US Army, 1926–30) quickly concluded that the French 75 was ineffective as a divisional support weapon. He urged that the development of a 105mm howitzer begin as soon as possible. His superiors at the time ignored his recommendation.

Following the First World War, the Westervelt Board also suggested it would be wise for the army to push along the development of a towed 105mm howitzer. The board's recommendation met with resistance because of the project's estimated expense.

Another problem was the fact that the army still had thousands of towed French 75s in the inventory as well as huge stocks of ammunition for the weapon. With limited funding available, many saw no reason to replace a perfectly serviceable existing weapon (despite its shortcomings in range and current battlefield ineffectiveness) with a yet-to-be-proven new cannon.

Field Artillery 105mm Howitzer

Despite the overall lack of interest in a 105mm howitzer from many senior army officers, the Ordnance Department drew up specifications in 1920 and began the development of a new horse-drawn 105mm howitzer labeled the M1 105mm Howitzer. It was accepted into service (standardized) in 1928 but never ordered into production. The design, however, was saved in case a situation warranted its production.

The Ordnance Department's lack of progress in developing a successful towed 105mm howitzer design spurred the army's Field Artillery Board to take matters into its own hands. The board began testing German 105mm towed howitzers from the First World War. The German howitzers performed so well that the Field Artillery Board recommended their adoption for service use.

The chief of the Ordnance Department denied the request. He claimed that the cost of reconditioning 300 captured German howitzers and a shortage of ammunition for those same cannons made the idea impractical. Instead, the Ordnance Department announced that an American-designed 105mm towed howitzer (based on the best features of the German 105mm howitzer) would go into development.

Fourteen prototypes of a revised version of the 105mm Howitzer M1 went out for testing between 1928 and 1933, intended for towing by wheeled vehicles. A successful example was finally developed in 1934 by the Ordnance Department and assigned the designation 105mm Howitzer

M2. In 1939, the Ordnance Department ordered forty-eight slightly modified examples of the M2, which became the M2A1.

Frustration

Despite the 105mm Howitzer M2A1's clear superiority over the obsolete French 75s still in inventory, the army's senior leadership continued to prefer modernizing the latter to spending money on acquiring the new howitzer. Congress proved so irritated by this stance that it tried to eliminate existing funding for modernization of the French 75 program in 1939. Congress's frustration appears in a Senate sub-committee on appropriation:

> The 75mm gun is being supplanted in foreign armies with the 105mm weapon, which has greater range and fires a heavier missile. Our Ordnance Department is developing such a gun and, undoubtedly, will be ready for production. If that is to be the weapon of the future,

---

Field Artillery Missions

From a February 1944 US Army Manual on the field artillery are the various types of fire missions assigned:

1. **Neutralization**: Fire delivered on areas to destroy the combat efficiency of enemy personnel by causing severe losses and interrupting movement or action. Neutralization is established by delivering surprise fire in intense masses. It is maintained by intermittent bursts of fire in lesser amounts.
2. **Destruction**: Fire delivered for the sole purpose of destroying material objects. It requires, except when direct laying is used, a great deal of ammunition and time. Observation is essential. For the destruction of most targets, medium and heavy artillery are better suited than is light artillery. Fire is generally by one gun.
3. **Registration**: Fire delivered to obtain corrections for increasing the accuracy of initial and subsequent fires.
4. **Harassing**: Fire delivered during relatively quiet periods, to lower enemy combat efficiency by keeping his troops unnecessarily alerted. Fire may be by single piece, platoon or battery; the fire is intermittent. All echelons of artillery may fire harassing fire.
5. **Interdiction**: Fire delivered on points or areas to prevent the enemy from using them. Characteristic targets are roads used for moving supplies or reserves, crossroads, assembly areas, railroad stations, detraining points, defiles, bridges and fords.

the committee questions the wisdom of continuing to spend large sums on the old 75.

It was not until France fell in June 1940 that the US Army made a concentrated effort to replace the French 75s with the new 105mm Howitzer M2A1. The M2A1, so long in gestation, would go on to become the chief divisional workhorse artillery piece of the US Army and the US Marine Corps, with 8,536 built by the end of the Second World War. Some of the French 75s remained in the army's inventory until 1943; when a sufficient number of M2A1s had entered service, the 75s were retired.

A Smaller and Lighter 105mm Howitzer

A more compact and lighter towed version of the 105mm Howitzer M2A1 was designated the 105mm Howitzer M3. Due to a shorter barrel, the weapon was sometimes referred to by unofficial nicknames such as the 'snub-nosed 105' or the 'sawed-off 105'. The M3 fired a semi-fixed round weighing 33lb, with a maximum range of approximately 5 miles.

The development of the M3 began in late 1941, reflecting the army's desire to have a lightweight counterpart available to formations where its attributes would prove useful. Some went to the army's airborne divisions to supplement their 75mm Pack Howitzers M1A1.

The majority of the 2,850 examples of the 105mm Howitzer M3, constructed between 1942 and 1944, therefore went to the newly-formed infantry cannon companies authorized in April 1942. These were attached to each of the three infantry regiments in an infantry division. The US Army mobilized sixty-eight infantry divisions during the Second World War.

Neither the army nor the Marine Corps retained their 105mm Howitzer M3 inventory following the Second World War. The US Marine Corps also

---

Japanese Countermeasure

From a June 1944 issue of *Field Artillery Journal* is a passage on one of the methods employed by the Japanese to confuse American artillerymen:

These tricky Nips once stopped our fire over here by firing into our rear areas at the same time we were firing. I knew none of our fire had fallen short, for I could see every volley, but it took some convincing to get going again. One observer joked that one Jap 90mm mortar fired at the right place and time could neutralize a whole division artillery. The liaison officer's job in such cases is to use his head and be intelligent enough to recognize such a ruse.

adopted the 105mm Howitzer M3 late in the war to supplement its 75mm Howitzer M1A1s. Most went to friendly countries under Military Assistance Programs in the immediate post-war period.

Self-Propelled 105mm Howitzer

An early attempt to place the 105mm Howitzer M2A1 on a self-propelled mount resulted in the production of 324 examples of what received the designation T19 105mm HMC. Like the weapon in the T30 75mm HMC, the M2A1 rode on the M3 series armored half-track with the howitzer mounted in a fixed forward position with limited traverse. The vehicle would see service in both North Africa and Sicily until replaced by a full-tracked vehicle.

The replacement for the T19 105mm HMC was the M7 105mm HMC, nicknamed the 'Priest' by the British as its machine-gun mount reminded them of European church pulpits. It consisted of the 105mm Howitzer M2A1 mounted on the open-topped chassis of an M3 medium tank in a fixed forward-firing position with limited traverse. The first example rolled off the factory floor in April 1942. Production of the M7 continued until the end of the Second World War, with a total of 3,490 built.

Improving the Vehicle

A second version of the vehicle went onto the open-topped chassis of the M4A3 version of the M4 series of medium tanks, receiving the designation M7A1. Again, the 105mm Howitzer M2A1 resided in a fixed forward-firing position with limited traverse. Production of the M7A1 totaled 826 examples, with the last vehicle completed in February 1945. They first entered front-line service in the summer of 1944 with various armored divisions.

In a Second World War US Army intelligence report, an American general commented on his division's impression of the M7:

> We have been in combat 63 days with the M7s and during that time we have had very few weapons out on account of motor trouble. Their extreme mobility has been very useful in the terrain and especially in the Cherbourg campaign and the breakthrough. I like them, and the men like them.

The 105mm Howitzer in a Tank

To overcome the disadvantage of mounting the 105mm Howitzer M2A1 in an open-topped chassis with limited traverse, the Ordnance Department decided to place the weapon inside the fully-enclosed, fully-rotating armored turret of two versions of the M4 series medium tank, the M4 and M4A3. A total of 1,641 examples of the former left the factory floor between February 1944 and March 1945, and 3,039 examples of the latter between May 1944 and June 1945.

In an April 1944 US Army document titled *Report of the New Weapon Board* is an extract praising the concept of self-propelled artillery:

The distinct advantage of self-propelled artillery over towed artillery is its ability to move into position and to move out before German counterbattery work can be affected. Even artillery officers previously opposed self-propelled artillery now agree that it has advantages for certain uses, that it is necessary, and that present self-propelled carriage design, mobility and dependability make the development of additional self-propelled mounts highly desirable.

The 155mm Howitzer Update

In recommending the development of a new 105mm light howitzer for divisional use, the Westervelt Board had discounted the need for a divisional 155mm medium support howitzer. The French-built 155mm M1917 and 1917A1 medium howitzers and the American copy designated the 155mm Howitzer M1918 were pulled from divisional service in 1920.

In 1929, the army decided to reinstate the 155mm howitzer in the TO&E (table of organization and equipment) of its infantry divisions. In 1933, Army Chief of Staff General Douglas MacArthur decided to have 600 examples of the 155mm Howitzer M1918 modernized, out of the approximately 3,000 in the inventory. In that time, the word motorization also meant modernization.

The first upgrading program for the 155mm Howitzer M1918 took place between 1936 and 1940, with the modified pieces acquiring the designation M1918A1. Additional improvements resulted in the designations M1918A2 and eventually the M1918A3 version. The army decided to have

1,414 further examples of the M1918 brought up to the M1918A3 standard by 1942, awaiting the introduction of a brand-new 155mm howitzer.

The modernization process involved equipping the guns' carriages with pneumatic tires for towing by prime movers rather than by horse teams. Such conversions received the label 'high-speed'. By 1939, 68 percent of the army's field artillery pieces were vehicle-towed and, by 1941, 100 percent were vehicle-towed or self-propelled.

The Upgrading Continues

At the same time, the decision came about to modernize the 155mm Howitzer M1918. A portion of the army's inventory of French 75s also received funding for modernization. Eventually, a total of 605 examples went through the process by 1941 and were re-designated as the 75mm Gun M1897, A2 through A4 versions. Other than training duties before America's official entry into the Second World War, none would go overseas to see combat. The US Army also had a portion of its inventory of 155mm Gun M1918A1 modernized for high-speed towing with the addition of pneumatic tires.

Also a decision appeared to modernize a portion of the US Army's pre-First World War inventory of light field artillery pieces: the 75mm gun Model 1916 and the 75mm gun Model 1917. The former became the M1916A1 and the latter the M1917A1. A few of the M1916A1s and M1917s saw combat in the Philippines, with others going overseas as military aid.

McNair's Input

Brigadier General Lesley J. McNair (eventually rising to the rank of lieutenant general) suggested in the 1930s that the army had placed too much importance on field artillery in the close support role for the infantry. McNair believed that modern long-range medium artillery pieces massing their fire together on important targets could be supremely effective on the battlefields of the future. McNair, therefore, urged that the army's infantry divisions reduce the number of light guns and howitzers (105mm and below) and increase the number of medium howitzers.

Field tests conducted by the US Army in 1937 confirmed McNair's belief that the 155mm howitzers, M1917 and M1918, were still superior to the new prototype 105mm Howitzer M2 due to their ability to deliver more explosives both on target and at longer ranges. Additional tests done in 1938 and information on foreign medium artillery development further emphasized the requirement for 155mm howitzers in the army's infantry divisions.

The Eyes of the Artillery

The first aerial observers were civilians that went up in balloons on behalf of the Union Army starting in 1861. Not impressed with the results, the Union Army ended its interactions with the civilian balloonists in 1863. Observation balloons reappeared in service during the First World War, with the US Army supplying the balloonists. Results were not that impressive with the lighter-than-air balloons. Aircraft seemed to offer a higher degree of usefulness as a platform from which artillery forward observers (FOs) could provide spotting information.

Holding back the implementation of aerial FOs within the US Army during the interwar period, besides internal disinterest, was the lack of a suitable aircraft and more modern radio equipment. The solution to the aircraft problem appeared in the late 1930s with the development and production of small, lightweight planes for the civilian market. In 1939, there was a technological breakthrough with the appearance of the first static-free radios due to the discovery of frequency modulation (FM), along with crystal control, allowing for push-button operation.

The aircraft eventually selected for the army was a militarized version of the two-man Cub J-3, both designed and built by the Piper Aircraft Corporation. Its military designation became the L-4. The army eventually acquired approximately 1,500 examples by the end of the Second World War.

Various unofficial nicknames for the L-4s soon appeared, including 'grasshoppers' and 'flying jeeps'. Each army field artillery firing battalion received two of the L-4s, with both the pilots who flew them and the mechanics who kept them flying belonging to the field artillery branch.

The New 155mm Towed Howitzer

A few days after the French surrender to the Germans in June 1940, the US Army adopted a new infantry division TO&E, which included four artillery battalions: three direct support (light) batteries of 105mm howitzers (eighteen pieces each) and one general support (medium) battalion of 155mm howitzers (twelve pieces). The 155mm howitzer would also be adopted into service by the US Marine Corps.

The cannon selected by the Ordnance Department for the general support battery in the new infantry division structure was the 155mm Howitzer M1. The Ordnance Department had begun developmental work on the weapon in 1920, but funding cuts meant that none would ever exist. In 1939, work on the weapon commenced once again and successful testing led to its standardization in May 1941.

Production of the 155mm Howitzer M1 began in October 1942. By the time the Second World War concluded, a total of 10,300 had rolled off the assembly lines. Enough of the new 155mm howitzers had reached the field by 1944 that the 155mm Howitzer M1918A3 found itself pulled from front-line service. American artillerymen affectionately referred to the old howitzer as a 'faithful old dog'.

The 155mm Howitzer M1 was often referred to by American cannoneers as 'the sweetest weapon on the front' due to its outstanding accuracy. The M1 fired a roughly 100lb separate-loaded round, having a maximum range of about 9 miles.

An example of the 155mm Howitzer M1 effectiveness in combat appears in the following passage from an article in the January/February 1992 issue of the *Field Artillery* magazine concerning the Battle of Manila, which took place between February and March 1945:

> US forces quickly discovered that 105mm fire against well-constructed structures [concrete] was ineffective. Usually, 155mm howitzers had to be brought up to within 200 to 400 yards of the building to pound the target. Often un-fuzed 155-mm shells were initially fired against large buildings to open cracks in the structure since such rounds dug deeper before exploding. Next, 155-mm rounds with delay fuzes would be fired into the weakened part of the target to widen the breach. Depending on whether a building was to be stormed or simply destroyed would dictate whether the cannoneers aimed for the top or bottom floor.

A number of the 155mm Howitzer M1 were sent out under Lend-Lease, with Great Britain receiving the largest number: 236 examples. Efforts made by the US Army to develop a self-propelled version of the 155mm M1 did not come to fruition until after the Second World War.

Odd Man Out

A 119mm (4.7in) to 127mm (5in) gun that would fit onto the same carriage proposed for what eventually became the 155mm Howitzer M1 came out of the Westervelt Board. However, like almost all the board's recommended artillery pieces, nothing came of it until the 1930s. As the gun's design progressed, a decision came about to make it a 114mm (4.5in) gun.

Production of the weapon designated the 4.5in gun M1 did not begin until September 1942. It fired a separate round weighing around 55lb, with a maximum range of approximately 12 miles.

Why the 4.5in gun M1 went into production remains unclear, as it was not as effective as the 155mm howitzer M1 and fired non-standard

Pictured here is a Napoleon smoothbore gun/howitzer at a Civil War battlefield site. It was the most numerous cannon in service with the Union Army during the American Civil War and the Confederate Army employed both captured examples as well as copies built in Southern foundries. The weapon also went by other labels, including the 12-pounder Model 1857 and the light 12-pounder gun. (*Public domain*)

(**Above**) Pictured here is the *Matériel de 75mm Modèle 1897*, a French-designed and built cannon that saw widespread use with the US Army during the First World War. American artillerymen referred to it as the 'French 75' or the '75'. The cannon proved to be the world's first modern artillery piece due to its hydro-pneumatic recoil mechanism. (*Pierre-Olivier Buan*)

(**Opposite, above**) Shown here during an interwar training exercise is a 3in anti-aircraft gun M3. It entered service in 1928 and would be the US Army's and Marine Corps' first-line air-defense weapon in the Second World War until replaced by a new generation of more capable and advanced anti-aircraft guns. A well-trained crew could fire up to twenty-five rounds per minute to an altitude of almost 21,000ft. (*Public domain*)

(**Opposite, below**) A French heavy howitzer adopted by the US Army in the First World War was the *Canon de 155 C Modèle 1917 Schneider*. In US Army service, it became the 155mm howitzer Model 1917; an American license-built version designated the 155mm howitzer Model 1918 is seen here. The pneumatic tires were added in the late 1930s to allow for towing by wheeled vehicles. (*Pierre-Olivier Buan*)

(**Above**) For its armored divisions, the US Army required a fully-tracked, self-propelled 105mm howitzer, which resulted in fielding of the M7 series of Howitzer Motor Carriages (HMCs). The original production units rode on a much-modified M3 medium tank chassis, with later examples such as the model shown here riding on an M4 series medium tank chassis labeled the M7B1. (*Public domain*)

(**Opposite, above**) The counterpart to the 155mm gun M1A1 nicknamed the 'Long Tom' is the 8in howitzer M1 pictured here. Both weapons used the same carriage. Although the howitzer had approval for production in 1938, an interwar budget shortfall delayed production until in 1940 the American government realized sooner or later it would find itself involved in the Second World War. By the end of the conflict, American factories had built 1,006 examples of the weapon. (*Public domain*)

(**Opposite, below**) Going onto a semi-truck trailer is a preserved example of the 75mm Howitzer Motor Carriage (HMC) M8, of which 1,778 examples came off the assembly lines between September 1942 and January 1944. In the US Army, the vehicle was assigned to armored cavalry squadrons to provide close-in fire support when needed against enemy defensive positions or unarmored targets. (*Christophe Vallier*)

(**Opposite, above**) It was clear to the US Army following the Second World War that all its self-propelled artillery pieces required overhead armor protection. An example of that belief appeared in 1952 as the M55 8in self-propelled howitzer, pictured here. Its 155mm counterpart was the M53 155mm self-propelled gun, which rode on the same chassis. The cannons were interchangeable, requiring only the rearrangement of ammunition storage. (*Pierre-Olivier Buan*)

(**Opposite, below**) Seen here is an M53 armed with a 155mm gun. Operated by a crew of six, the armored protection on the vehicle would protect it only from small-arms fire and artillery fragments. The vehicle had storage space onboard for 20 rounds. (*Chris Hughes*)

(**Above**) The introduction of the M41 Walker Bulldog light tank in the early 1950s resulted in the withdrawal from service of the Second World War-era M24 Chaffee light tank. The twin 40mm gun mount from the 40mm Gun Motor Carriage (GMC) (based on the M24 light tank), came off and was placed on the modified chassis of the M41, leading to the introduction of the M42 40mm self-propelled anti-aircraft gun pictured here. (*Richard and Barb Eshleman*)

(**Above**) Seen here during the Vietnam War is a Marine Corps M101A1 105mm howitzer, which had been labeled the M2A1 during the Second World War. The nomenclature system had changed in 1962. Due to its light weight, it was a favorite during the conflict as it was easily transported as a helicopter sling load to locations that were otherwise inaccessible to towed or self-propelled artillery batteries. (*Public domain*)

(**Opposite, above**) The 105mm howitzer M2A1/M101's larger and more powerful Second World War towed counterpart, the 155mm howitzer M1, enjoyed a long second career with both the US Army and Marine Corps. In 1962, it was re-designated the M114, with an example pictured here during a training exercise. Like the M101, the M114 would go on to see service with many foreign armies when the American military pulled them from service and offered them as military aid. (*Public domain*)

(**Opposite, below**) A diorama built around an M108 self-propelled howitzer armed with a 105mm howitzer. Unlike the M53 and M55, the M108 had 360 degrees traverse. Introduced in the early 1960s, it saw combat during the Vietnam War. (*Pierre-Olivier Buan*)

(**Opposite**) Reaching operational status with the US Army in 1958 was the Nike Hercules ground-to-air missile pictured here. It was a much upgraded and modernized version of the previous-generation missile known as the Nike Ajax, which entered service in 1953. The Nike Ajax had only a high-explosive warhead to down high-flying enemy aircraft, however, the Nike Hercules had a nuclear warhead to destroy incoming enemy bomber formations. (*Chris Hughes*)

(**Above**) Taking part in a Marine Corps training exercise is the M110A2 8in self-propelled howitzer. The muzzle brake identifies it as an A2 variant. The original version and the follow-on M110A1 did not have muzzle brakes. The M110 series entered service in 1963 with both the US Army and the Marine Corps. There was also the M107 175mm self-propelled gun, built on the same chassis. Neither remains in service with the American military. (*Public domain*)

(**Above**) One of the more abject US Army acquisition failures proved to be the M247 Sergeant York Division Air Defense (DIVAD), a self-propelled anti-aircraft gun (SPAAG), one of which is seen here. Developed in the late 1970s, its intended role was to protect the army's M1 Abrams tanks and M2/M3 Bradley Infantry Fighting Vehicles (IFVs) from Soviet ground-attack aircraft and attack helicopters. With endless technical design problems and large cost overruns, it was canceled in 1985. (*Public domain*)

(**Opposite, above**) Taking part in a training exercise, a US Army artilleryman is loading a round into an M102 105mm howitzer. Developed as a lightweight replacement for the M2A1/M101 105mm howitzer for the army's airborne units, the M102 can be sling-loaded and transported by helicopters and also air-dropped by parachute. The M102's reduced weight came from the use of an aluminum carriage. (*Public domain*)

(**Opposite, below**) The M109 155mm self-propelled howitzer pictured here initially entered US Army service in 1963. Rather than depending on the chassis and suspension components from the army's tanks, the M109 consists of a specially-designed chassis and turret made from aluminum alloy armor to keep the vehicle's weight down, as with all the army's long line of post-war self-propelled artillery pieces. (*Public domain*)

(**Opposite, above**) The Honest John rocket pictured proved to be the US Army's first nuclear-armed, surface-to-surface, unguided rocket. Entering US Army service in 1953, it deployed to Western Europe the following year. With a length of 27 feet 3-inches, the approximately 6,000lb weapon, in its initial iteration, had a range of around 15 miles. Besides a 20-kiloton nuclear warhead, there existed a 1,500lb conventional high-explosive warhead for the rocket. (*Richard and Barb Eshleman*)

(**Opposite, below**) On display is a preserved example of the Lance missile. It entered into US Army service in 1972, as a replacement for the Honest John rocket, and the Corporal missile, the latter having entered service in 1954. The 20-foot long missile weighed approximately 3,000lbs and had an inertial guidance system. Range depended on the warhead fitted, either nuclear or conventional, with a maximum range up to 75 miles. (*Richard and Barb Eshleman*)

(**Above**) In this picture, we see a Marine Corps 155mm howitzer, designated as the M777, at the moment of firing. Notice the projectile leaving the muzzle. The British-designed and built weapon entered American military service in 2005, as the replacement for the older-generation M198 towed 155mm howitzer. With conventional unguided rounds, it has a maximum range of about 18 miles. With the extended range, Excalibur round the top range rises to approximately 25 miles. (*Marine Corps*)

The nuclear-armed Pershing missile seen here launched during a test flight entered US Army service in 1963. The 34.5-foot missile weighed in at approximately 10,000lbs, and with an inertial guidance system could reach targets at a range of up to 460 miles. With the authorization for a much-improved model of the missile in 1965. The initial model became the Pershing 1, with the upgraded version designated as the Pershing 1a. (*Public Domain*)

ammunition rounds, creating logistical issues. In the end, the production of the weapon was limited to only 426 examples. They did, however, see combat in Western Europe, with almost all scrapped shortly after the Second World War.

The Long Tom

One of the weapons that received the most praise from artillerymen interviewed after the First World War by the Westervelt Board was the French-designed and built *Canon de 155 Grande Puissance Filloux Modèle 1917*, commonly referred to by American artillerymen as the 'GPF'. Hence the Westervelt Board recommended that the Ordnance Department develop an improved, longer-ranged version of the weapon, intended for use as a corps-level weapon and not a divisional weapon.

Unfortunately, like the other artillery pieces suggested by the Westervelt Board, the curtailment of artillery research funds in 1921 temporarily ended work on a new towed 155mm gun. Development work on the weapon began again in the 1930s, leading to its standardization in July 1938 as the 155mm gun M1.

The New and Improved 155mm Gun

Production of the M1 began in October 1940, and after the first twenty examples came off the assembly lines, some minor changes resulted in the revised designation of 155mm Gun M1A1. By the war's end, a total of 1,882 had come off the factory floor.

Most American soldiers and Marines referred to the 155mm Gun M1A1 by its unofficial nickname of the 'Long Tom'. The weapon first saw action in North Africa in 1942/43 with the US Army. In the January 1944 issue of the *Field Artillery Journal* is the following extract describing what captured German prisoners said about the weapon:

> The Germans come in and say they cower with fear when the rifle [Long Tom] is finding them. They say they can tell a 155 shell. They can see the [muzzle] flash 10 miles away and hear the report [sound], and then nothing happens for what seems like several minutes. But they know it's coming ... All they know is a lot of explosives is somewhere far away and descending on them.

Captured enemy soldiers were so impressed by the weapon's sustained rate of fire (one round per minute or a battery burst rate of four or five rounds per minute) that they asked to see what they believed was an automatic-loading artillery piece. The Long Tom fired a separate-loaded round weighing around 95lb with a maximum range of around 15 miles.

New Towed 8in Howitzer

Based on the same towed carriage as the Long Tom was the 8in Howitzer M1. A slightly different version labeled the M2 appeared in 1945. The new 8in howitzer was the replacement for the British-designed and built heavy howitzers adopted by the US Army during the First World War. The army standardized the weapon in 1938, with the first production examples ordered in June 1940.

The 8in howitzer entered into field service in 1942. It fired a 200lb separate-loaded round, with a maximum range of approximately 10 miles. Including post-war-built units, a total of 1,006 came off the factory floor.

Self-Propelled Heavy Artillery Pieces

The chief of ordnance came up with an innovative idea in the summer of 1941. He suggested mounting surplus First World War-era 155mm gun

Time On Target

One of the most impressive accomplishments of the US Army field artillery employed during the Second World War came to be known as 'Time On Target', shortened to the acronym 'TOT'. It was a method of massing fire of numerous artillery batteries (with different types of cannons located at various sites) on a single target, with all the rounds landing at approximately the same time.

As most enemy casualties occurred in the first few seconds, timing all rounds to arrive in the shortest time possible markedly increased effectiveness. It was an interwar development by the US Army's Field Artillery School, reinforced by British experience in North Africa.

At Elsenborn Ridge, during the Battle of the Bulge, the US 1st, 2nd, 9th and 99th Infantry Divisions could call on twenty-three corps and divisional batteries, plus thirty-six regimental batteries. The total of 348 corps, divisional and regimental artillery pieces, plus 4.2in chemical mortars delivered devastating TOTs, possibly the largest American concentration of the war.

The key component that made TOT possible was the interwar development of the battalion-level Fire Direction Center (FDC). It was staffed by the most experienced artillerymen, who took over the time-consuming and challenging task of making the calculations and plotting required to engage targets, a role formerly performed by individual artillery battery commanders.

The FDC relied on ground-based forward observers (FOs) equipped with radios and field telephones and aerial observers to observe the fall of rounds and provide any necessary fire adjustments. In a March 1945 memo, a US Army general commented on the effectiveness of FDCs during the Italian campaign (1943–45), which allowed for the 'massing of fires up to seven battalions after the adjustment [of] observed fire by one battalion, or by one forward observer' to become routine.

In the September 1946 issue of *Field Artillery Journal* appears a quote in an article titled 'Heroes' regarding artillery forward observers: 'There wasn't a man at the front who wasn't happy to see an artilleryman,' Captain Owen R. O'Neill of the 383rd Infantry Regiment said when asked what his men thought about forward observers. 'If they weren't around, the men were jittery. It didn't make any difference whether it was an enlisted man or an officer, just as long as it was an artilleryman. They were the greatest single morale factor we had at the front.' The job of the forward observers came with an elevated risk of becoming a casualty. They were considered high-priority targets by all sides.

barrels on the open-topped chassis of modified M3 series medium tanks, creating a simple and very cost-effective self-propelled artillery piece.

A prototype designated the T6 Gun Motor Carriage (GMC) showed up in February 1942. In a comparison test between the T6 and a towed 155mm gun, the former moved 6 miles to a new firing position in only thirty-five minutes; the latter took more than three hours to reach the same location.

Despite a lack of interest by the Army Ground Forces (AGF) in a self-propelled 155mm gun, the Ordnance Department continued to see a promising future for the weapon. In March 1942, the Ordnance Department standardized the T6, which then became the M12 GMC. The first production vehicles appeared in September 1942. It took until late 1943 when the army began specifying the equipment needed for the planned invasion of France that the M12 started to interest the AGF.

The first M12s arrived in France in July 1944, with the vehicle coming into its own in the fall of 1944 as the US Army came up against the German Siegfried Line's massive fortifications. It found itself quickly pushed into the role of pillbox-buster. An example shows up in an article titled 'An M12 Battalion in Combat' that appeared in the January 1945 issue of the *Field Artillery Journal*:

> Based on the experiences so far gained, we believe that the M12, suitably employed, will destroy, penetrate, or knock out of action pillboxes of the Siegfried Line type. The projectile produces casualties and lowers the morale of the pillbox occupants. No penetrations on the heavy 14″ steel cupolas which the better pillboxes have are known of. It is also difficult to penetrate the best type of concrete, but in some cases, 7ft of concrete were penetrated fairly easily. Final conclusions must await further experiences.

240mm Howitzer and 8in Gun

The largest towed field artillery pieces placed into production for the US Army during the Second World War included the 240mm Howitzer M1 and the 8in Gun M1. Both fit onto near-identical carriages. Production of the 240mm howitzer and the 8in gun both began in 1942. Of the former, 315 were built and of the latter, 139.

In the 1930s, the US Army had expressed little interest in either the 240mm howitzer or the 8in gun. It would fall to the Ordnance Department to push their development along, anticipating a need for them in a future war. AGF interest in them spiked after the fighting in North Africa when German Army 170mm guns designated the *17-cm K18* appeared; these out-ranged the Long Toms.

Before America's involvement in the Second World War, the widespread belief among many senior army officers was that aircraft would take over the role once performed by heavy artillery. Unfortunately, this did not prove to be the case. Major General McNair would comment after an inspection visit to North Africa in May 1943: 'Instead of artillery becoming an arm which is tending to fade out of the picture under the pressure of airpower or tanks, it is here in the same strength and importance that it had in the [First] World War.'

Due to the great length of the 240mm and 8in cannons' barrels, neither could be towed in one piece. Therefore, the barrels and carriage were towed into position by separate vehicles and reassembled on-site with the aid of a mobile crane.

The 240mm howitzer fired a separate-loaded round that weighed 360lb, with a maximum range of around 14 miles. In the April 1945 issue of the *Field Artillery Journal*, in an article titled 'One Year of Combat with the 240s' is the following passage:

These howitzers have been used for everything from direct support of infantry troops (we chased Tiger tanks and four heavy machine guns one day with an observed mission) to the more normal general support missions of harassing and interdiction fires deep in enemy territory; counterbattery, both observed and unobserved; and – of prime importance – observed destruction missions.

The 8in Gun in Action

During the fighting in Italy, the US Army preferred the 8in gun as it was longer-ranged, firing a separate-loaded round weighing 240lb with a maximum range of 20 miles. From an April 1944 US Army document titled *Report of the New Weapons Board*:

The 8" gun is generally needed in the Italian theater. Almost all the artillery in that theater is now massed along the front lines. Because of their long range, 8" guns can be emplaced in the rear of this massed artillery and thus used more effectively. In addition, their long range would be capable of reaching out as far as any German weapon now in use in that theater. At the present time, our combat units are being outranged by the German 17cm gun.

By the Rocket's Red Glare

Another artillery weapon that found a small niche with both the US Army and the Marine Corps during the Second World War was the rocket. However, it took until 1943 and widespread use by the German and Red

Army before rockets attracted any interest. An advantage of rockets appears in an Ordnance Department manual dated February 1944 on rockets and their launchers: 'Of tremendous importance in considering the advantages of rockets are the ease and cheapness of manufacture of the launcher in comparison with the complexity and high cost of a gun. The rocket-launcher is simply a guide and consists either of a tube or parallel tracks.'

What the US Army eventually fielded in 1944 were six battalions of three batteries each; each battery equipped with twelve T27 rocket-launchers. Only one battalion made it to Europe before the German surrender and took part in a single engagement. The rockets themselves were 4.5in (114mm), designated the M8 series. The T27 rocket-launchers could be placed on the ground and fired or fired from trucks. The M8 rocket had a range of around 2 miles.

The 4.5in launcher units themselves varied in the number of tubes. The T27 truck and ground-mounted models had eight tubes, and a version adapted to fire from the turret of an M4 series medium tank, designated the T34, had sixty tubes. The Marine Corps first employed makeshift truck-mounted rocket-launchers firing the M8 series rockets during the Battle for Saipan in June 1944 and then at Tinian between July and August 1944.

A New Rocket

In April 1945, the improved M16 4.5in rocket began replacing the M8 series rockets. It came with a new two-wheeled trailer designated the T66 Launcher, which consisted of twenty-four tubes and received the nickname 'Honeycomb'. The M16 rocket had a maximum range of around 3 miles.

The Honeycomb would go on to see combat in only one engagement with the US Army at the very end of the war in Europe. In an article titled 'Artillery Rockets' which appeared in the October 1946 issue of the *Field Artillery Journal*, the author stated:

> A rocket battery battalion can fire an 864-round volley, the equivalent of seventy-two battalions of 105mm howitzers firing a one-volley TOT. And while a single rocket-launcher is less accurate than a single cannon, a battery rocket volley is about as accurate as a TOT fired by a number of cannon battalions.

Despite this advantage, the army was not impressed at the time with its rocket artillery as it proved too short-ranged and inaccurate compared to tube artillery.

The M16 4.5in rocket also came with a fourteen-tube launcher designated the T44, designed to fire from light trucks. The first unit so equipped belonged to the Marine Corps and saw combat during the invasion of Iwo Jima in January 1944. A nickname applied to those who served in the Marine rocket detachments was the 'Buck Rogers Men'.

Anti-Aircraft Artillery

The First World War witnessed the birth of aerial warfare. To deal with this new battlefield threat, the US Army's senior leadership gave the job to the Coast Artillery Branch in 1917. They, therefore, modified two of their existing 3in (75mm) seacoast defense guns for the air defense role. Reflecting on their new jobs, one became the Anti-Aircraft Artillery (AAA) Gun Model 1917 and the other the AAA Gun M1918.

Due to its size and weight, the M1917 was intended only for static positions, guarding US Navy bases and important American seaports. The lighter and smaller M1918 was to be mounted on a towed trailer to accompany US Army units sent to fight in France. An order for 612 examples of the M1918 went on the books in 1917, but in the end, none made it overseas during the First World War.

In the years following the First World War, the development of the next generation of AAA guns went nowhere. There was a lack of funding, accompanied by the short-sighted belief among some senior army officers that ground-attack aircraft had been only a fad. The army's infantry division commanders believed that their existing machine guns were more than capable of dealing with hostile aircraft and did not require the attachment of Coast Artillery AAA units.

Improving the Existing Weapons

In the meantime, the Ordnance Department decided to improve the Coast Artillery's First World War-era AAA inventory. With some improvements, the 3in AAA Gun Model 1917 became the 3in AAA Gun M2 and later the M4. Their size and weight restricted them to fixed mounts at Coast Artillery fortifications. They would last in service through the Second World War before they all went off to scrappers.

For field use, the Ordnance Department came up with a much-improved mobile 3in AAA Gun M1918. The reworked weapon found itself standardized in 1927 as the 3in AAA Gun M3, with about 800 in army service by 1940. A modified version of the gun became the main armament of the US Army M10 Tank Destroyer.

The 3in AAA Gun M3 was reasonably effective against military aircraft of the 1920s. Unfortunately, it proved obsolete against the faster, higher-flying aircraft of the 1930s but remained in US Army service through the Second World War. It fired a roughly 25lb fixed round, able to reach an altitude of about 26,000ft, although effective fire above 20,000ft was considered extremely poor.

By the late 1930s, as the Spanish Civil War (1936–39) raged, America's military and political leaders began urging that funding be made available to upgrade the US Army's weaponry, including the AAA guns of the Coast Artillery. At the same time, the army's leadership still believed that there was no need to attach Coast Artillery AAA battalions to its infantry divisions.

AAA Detection

In 1939 radar (originally an acronym of the words 'Radio Detection and Ranging') was still in its infancy and not yet in field use with AAA units. To detect and locate hostile aircraft in darkness AAA units employed powerful searchlights. Within the army, the searchlight units were affectionately called either 'moonlight cavalry' or 'smoothbore artillery'.

In 1939 Coast Artillery AAA units still depended on primitive sound detection devices mounted on a wheeled trailer to give warning of enemy aircraft flying at night. The first sound detection devices were placed into service by the French Army during the First World War and consisted of nothing more than huge horns with a microphone fitted within.

With these first crude instruments, trained listeners could tell the approximate direction from which enemy aircraft were approaching. That information went off to searchlight control system operators, who would point the searchlights in the general direction indicated. On a reasonably quiet and calm night, a sound detection device could pick up a noisy aircraft at a distance of up to 20 miles. A well-trained crew could also determine an estimate of the aircraft's direction and altitude.

AAA Radar

British scientists, in June 1935, were the first to use radar to track aircraft. The US Army's Coast Artillery branch began pushing the senior leadership of the service in early 1936 to authorize the funding needed to incorporate radar into its inventory. By May of that same year, the US Army Signal Corps, assigned the responsibility for radar's development, finished a prototype. By 1940 production examples of the prototype radar system, now designated the SCR-268, were entering service.

The SCR-268 consisted of a mobile trailer-mounted system that had a maximum range of approximately 24 miles. Their mission was to locate enemy aircraft accurately enough for searchlights to instantly find them in the night sky. Dozens of SCR-268 radar sets went with US Army units during the Battle for North Africa (1942–43) and proved effective in many situations, but unfortunately were easily jammed by the enemy.

Gun-Laying Radar

With the limited success of the SCR-268, the next step was the development of a trailer-mounted radar not so easily jammed that could aim the guns of an AAA unit directly, without searchlights. Such a system in military terminology is a gun-laying radar. It must be able to determine the range, azimuth (compass direction) and elevation of a target with high precision to be effective.

The army's first production example of a new gun-laying radar, designated the SCR-584, appeared for testing in May 1943. Its combat debut occurred during the fighting for the Anzio beachhead in Italy in early 1944, where it enabled AAA gunners to play havoc with German aerial attacks.

The SCR-584 provided AAA units with the automatic tracking of both high- and low-flying enemy aircraft out to 27 miles, with an early warning range of 56 miles. The combat effectiveness of the SCR-584 soon won excellent reviews and resulted in its widespread demand throughout the remainder of the war.

Typically, the SCR-584 found itself tied into the army's mobile SCR-270 Long-Range Air Search surveillance radar units, with a range of approximately 270 miles. For inclement weather or darkness, a height-finding radar designated the SCR-547 eventually appeared in service to work alongside the SCR-584 and the SCR-270.

AAA Accessories

Before the wartime introduction of the SCR-547 height-finding radar, the army employed the M1A1 Optical Height Finder. It consisted of a 13.5ft-long stereoscopic range-finder that continuously determined the slant range and altitude of aircraft in clear weather and daytime conditions. (The slant range is the line of sight from a ground position to an aerial target.)

The data gathered by the M1A1 Optical Height Finder, or the SCR-547 Height-Finding Radar, at a large-caliber AAA unit went into the M9A1 Director, a primitive mechanical-electro (analog) computer with attached telescopes. It continuously provided the predicted flight paths of aircraft and furnishing fuze settings for multiple AAA guns. The individual gun crews aimed their weapons by watching the information provided by the M9A1 Director on dial pointers attached to their guns.

90mm Anti-Aircraft Gun

It took until 1940 before the US Army approved the creation of separate AAA battalions for attachment to its field divisions. The reason: the successful use of ground-attack aircraft by the German military in Poland and Western Europe. To come up with a new AAA gun, the Ordnance Department rushed the development of a 90mm (3.5in) AAA gun first proposed in 1938. It was standardized in February 1940 as the 90mm Gun M1.

The 90mm Gun M1 found itself succeeded by a slightly modified version labeled the M1A1. The final model could fire at ground targets as well as aerial targets and became the M2 version. It was not unheard-of for the weapon to be deployed as an artillery piece or as back-up anti-tank guns. The gun itself went into the M36 Tank Destroyer, as well as what eventually became the M26 Pershing Heavy Tank (later medium tank).

The 90mm AAA gun fired a fixed round weighing around 40lb, able to reach an altitude of about 43,000ft. A total of 6,648 examples of the 90mm AAA guns were built by 1945 and served overseas with both the US Army and the Marine Corps. Besides the anti-aircraft role, they proved useful in the ground support role, as appears in the following passage from the January–February 1948 issue of the *Coast Artillery Journal*:

> During World War II, commanders in all theaters realized and appreciated the possibilities of the 90mm anti-aircraft gun as a powerful

ground support weapon. It has lent itself particularly to the role of medium artillery in general support and reinforcing missions. It has demonstrated remarkable ability as a direct fire weapon, particularly against caves and pillboxes where its high muzzle velocity and flat trajectory may be exploited.

Besides the overseas AAA gun role, a large number went into service as seacoast defense guns during the Second World War. Stationed along both the East and West Coasts of the United States, some of them featured an armored shield for crew protection when engaging enemy vessels.

120mm Anti-Aircraft Gun

A fear that the enemy might produce a long-range four-engined bomber like the Army Air Force's B-29 Superfortress led to the fielding in February 1944 of a larger AAA gun. That weapon turned out to be the 120mm (4.7in) Gun M1, nicknamed the 'Stratosphere Gun'.

The Stratosphere Gun fired a separate-loaded round, having a practical ceiling of about 57,000ft. The M2 variant of the gun could reach 60,000ft. With a power rammer, the gun had an average rate of fire of ten rounds per minute. For unknown reasons, the 120mm round was less accurate

---

A New Artillery Fuze

In 1944, army AAA units began employing proximity fuzes, also known as VT fuzes and code-named 'POZIT'. It consisted of a miniature radio transmitter and receivers, powered by tiny battery cells. When proximity-fuzed projectiles came close to their intended targets, the radio waves sent out by the transmitter reflected back to the receiver in enough strength to close a circuit that initiated fuze action and caused a resulting explosion.

The advancement in technology provided by the proximity fuze dramatically improved the effectiveness of the army's AAA units for the remainder of the war. Before the introduction of the proximity fuze, large-caliber AAA guns used mechanical, spring-activated time fuzes.

Up until the Battle of the Bulge (December 1944–January 1945), proximity fuzes did not go to army artillery gun and howitzer units. The reason: fear that an example would fall into the hands of the Germans. General Dwight D. Eisenhower, however, overruled that decision.

The proximity-fuzed projectiles fired from US Army guns and howitzers during the Battle of the Bulge had a pre-burst feature set by artillerymen before firing, which would detonate the projectile above the ground anywhere between 2ft and 33ft, creating a very potent air-burst.

---

than the 90mm round. In traveling order, the Stratosphere weighed around 30 tons, almost as much as a first-generation M4 series medium tank.

Only 550 examples of the 120mm AAA gun came off the assembly lines before it became clear that America's enemies could not construct aircraft capable of reaching the United States. Except for a single firing battery deployed to Hawaii in 1945, all others remained Stateside, guarding important sites such as Washington DC. The 120mm AAA gun, like the 90mm AAA gun, would remain in service during the immediate post-war period.

Smaller-Caliber Anti-Aircraft Guns

German Army employment of specialized ground-attack aircraft early in the Second World War convinced most that the US Army's field divisions required a large number of short-range, fast-firing (automatic) weapons to engage low-flying enemy aircraft. The result: a variety of ground, trailer and vehicle-mounted multiple .50 caliber M2 machine-gun mounts.

Two trailer-mounted AAA guns appeared in army service during the Second World War: the Multiple Cal. .50 Machine Gun Carriage M51 and Multiple Cal. .50 Machine Gun Trailer Mount M55. The preferred vehicle mount came to be the M3 series of armored half-tracks. With two .50 caliber machine guns mounted on an electrically-powered turret, it became the M13 Multiple Gun Motor Carriage (MGMC).

The M3 series half-track armed with four .50 caliber machine guns became the M16 MGMC. When armed with two .50 caliber machine guns and a single 37mm AAA Gun M1A2, the vehicle became the M15 GMC, with an improved version designated the M15A1.

The 40mm Anti-Aircraft Gun

The prewar-developed and fielded 37mm AAA Gun M1A2 was not the preferred choice of the US Army and found itself replaced by the 40mm Automatic Gun M1, standardized in April 1941. The 40mm AAA gun would eventually replace all the 37mm AAA guns in the army's inventory by 1943.

The 40mm AAA gun fired an approximately 5lb round, with an effective ceiling of 19,000ft. The popular name of the weapon was 'Bofors' after the Swedish firm that had designed the gun. The American military had acquired license rights to build a modified version of the weapon.

For added mobility, the 40mm AAA gun went onto both M2 and M3 series armored half-tracks, as well as the modified chassis of the M4 series medium tank as experiments. None would go into production, however, although a few 40mm AAA guns were fitted on M3 armored half-tracks in

Australia as a field improvisation by a local Ordnance Department unit and these saw combat.

Seacoast Artillery

Following the First World War, the US Army's 10in and 12in guns returned to their coastal defense emplacements in the United States. At the same time, an effort began to modernize the country's existing seacoast artillery inventory. The first step was to remove all older-generation fixed guns considered obsolete. The process eventually encompassed ten different gun types totaling approximately 300 pieces, mostly the smaller-caliber guns.

To increase their range, older-generation 10in and 12in guns went onto new fixed barbette carriages allowing for elevation up to 65 degrees. The disappearing gun carriages had a maximum elevation of only 20 degrees. Due to interwar factors such as better-armed and armored battleships and the advent of the aircraft carrier, the Coast Artillery Corps began to rethink its weapon inventory.

There were two post-First World War additions to the Coast Artillery inventory in the 1920s, fitted onto near-identical carriages. These included the 16in gun Model 1919 and the 16in howitzer Model 1920. Due to a lack of funding, only seven of the former would go on to be built and emplaced, plus only four of the latter.

The 16in gun 1919 fired a 2,340lb round, having a maximum range of around 28 miles, and the 16in howitzer 1920 fired a 2,100lb round, having a maximum range of 14 miles.

In the July–August 1936 issue of the *Coast Artillery Journal* appears the following passage:

> Arguments are often heard as to the value of 16-inch long-range batteries for harbor defense. It is held by all who have given unbiased thought to the subject that the mere presence of long-range, high-powered batteries in a harbor defense will force a naval commander at least to hesitate, if not refuse, to bring his ships within their range.

US Navy-Supplied Guns

Supplementing the large older-generation seacoast artillery during the interwar period were US Navy 8in and 16in battleship guns that had become surplus to requirements with the signing of the Washington Naval Treaty of 1922. These guns went onto US Army-designed and built carriages. Of the forty-eight examples of the 8in Navy gun, some appeared on railroad mounts while others became fixed seacoast defense guns.

Of the seventy examples of the surplus Navy 16in guns, twenty went to the US Army between 1922 and 1924 and another forty-seven in January 1941. The Coast Artillery Corps had originally anticipated building twenty-seven new casemated batteries of two guns each, using the surplus Navy 16in guns, around essential seaports. Their assigned designation: the 16in Gun Mark II Model 1.

The Navy-supplied 16in guns were not as heavy as the seven examples of the Army's 16in gun M1919 constructed, hence their range was a bit shorter at 25 miles. They did, however, go onto a modified version of the carriage initially designed for the US Army 16in gun M1919.

By 1943, as the threat from foreign navies receded, the number of the 16in two-gun batteries went down to twenty-one. Of the twenty-one eventually constructed, not all were fitted with their guns as it became clear by 1944 that seacoast artillery was obsolete as a concept.

Railroad Seacoast Artillery

Some of the 300 or so 8in guns and 12in mortars constructed for use in the First World War were retained on their railroad cars. The Coast Artillery Corps deployed them in the US, Panama and Hawaii. All would go to the scrap dealers following the Second World War.

In the early 1920s, the Coast Artillery Corps took into service approximately twenty examples of a new 8in railroad gun fitted onto a US Army-designed railroad gun carriage. It received the designation 8in Gun Railroad Mount M1A1. Instead of an Army-designed gun it was a Navy-designed gun, which provided more range and accuracy than its Army counterpart.

The only other railroad guns constructed after the First World War were four examples of the 14in Gun Railroad Mount 1920. Two went to Los Angeles, California and two to the Panama Canal Zone. To fire the guns at enemy warships, they were removed from their railroad wheel assemblies and positioned over circular concrete blocks, which provided them with 360 degrees of traverse.

Tractor-Drawn Seacoast Artillery

As a back-up to the railroad seacoast artillery, there were the tractor-drawn medium-caliber artillery pieces, the most numerous being the 155mm Gun Model 1917 and 1918. To overcome the lack of lateral movement on its field carriage when called upon to engage enemy warships, the Coast Artillery Corps came up with the fixed concrete and steel 'Panama mount' in the 1920s.

Marine Corps Coastal Defense Guns

For its land-based defense battalions, first formed in the summer of 1939, the US Navy provided the Marine Corps with three types of surplus naval guns. Initially intended for shipboard use and converted into fixed seacoast guns, these included the 3in .50 Caliber Mk 21 Model 0, the 5in .51 Caliber Mk 15 Model 0 and the 7in .45 Caliber Mk 2 Model 0.

The 3in .50 gun and the 5in .51 gun were considered dual-purpose weapons, employed against both surface and aerial threats, whereas the 7in .45 gun had always been only an anti-ship weapon. It fired a 165lb round, with a maximum range of about 9 miles. Four were present at the Battle of Midway, crewed by the Marine Defense Battalion.

As the tide of the war in the Pacific turned against the Japanese, the value of the defense battalions considerably lessened with some disbanded in 1944 and others converted to anti-aircraft units. The naval-supplied guns employed in the coastal defense role were withdrawn from service and scrapped.

A description of what the mount offered appears in a US Army manual titled *Seacoast Artillery Weapons* dated October 1944:

> The advantages that this mount offers are that the gun retains its mobility, the emplacement is stable and firm, and the gun is able to engage a moving naval target throughout its assigned field of fire. Panama mounts may be emplaced to provide a 180-degree or 360-degree traverse, depending largely upon the mission assigned and the surrounding terrain.

In 1943 there appeared a movable all-steel version of the Panama mount for the Long Tom, nicknamed the 'Kelly mount' after its inventor, a Coast Artillery officer, Colonel P.E. Kelly.

The majority of the Coast Artillery Corps' seacoast defense artillery batteries – be they fixed, towed or railroad-mounted – were disbanded between 1944 and 1946, with most of their weaponry quickly scrapped.

(**Above**) The most modern artillery piece to appear in the US Army's inventory during the interwar period (1919–39) proved to be the 75mm pack howitzer. Designed to be broken down into six components which could be horse-transported, its original carriage had wooden wheels with steel rims. With the US Army's formation of airborne forces, a new carriage that rode on pneumatic tires appeared for the 75mm pack howitzer, as pictured here. (*Pierre-Olivier Buan*)

(**Opposite, above**) An M1A1 75mm pack howitzer is pictured here during a photo event staged by the US Army. Those assigned to the army's airborne divisions were in their glider infantry battalions. However, the weapon could be broken down into its various components and dropped by parachute if the need arose. The Marine Corps made widespread use of the 75mm pack howitzer as it proved much easier to move to firing positions inaccessible to the larger 105mm and 155mm howitzers. (*National Archives*)

(**Opposite, below**) With the formation of its first armored divisions in 1940, the US Army quickly realized it had an urgent need for self-propelled artillery. An early example of this requirement appeared in the form of the T30 75mm Howitzer Motor Carriage (HMC) pictured here. The vehicle would initially see service with the US Army during the fighting in North Africa (December 1942 through May 1943). They saw use in the army's armored reconnaissance units. (*Patton Museum*)

(**Above**) The wartime replacement for the T30 HMC turned out to be the M8 HMC shown here. The vehicle consisted of a modified M5 Light Tank chassis, with the M1A1 75mm pack howitzer installed in a specially-designed, open-topped turret. Production of the vehicle began in September 1942 and continued until January 1944, with a total of 1,778 examples completed. (*Pierre-Olivier Buan*)

(**Opposite, above**) With an extensive inventory of French 75s and not a lot of interwar funding, the US Army decided in the late 1930s to modernize a portion of their stockpile. The initial upgrades involved the addition of pneumatic tires as pictured here plus air brakes. Next came a new split trail carriage, which replaced the original pole trail. With these improvements the original French 75 (the 75mm gun Model 1875) became the 75mm field gun Model 1874A4. (*National Archives*)

(**Opposite, below**) A preserved example of a 105mm howitzer M2A1. It entered US Army service in 1940 and served almost everywhere the US Army and Marine Corps campaigned during the Second World War. By the time production ceased in 1953, a total of 10,202 examples had come off the factory floor. It weighed in at around 5,000lb and fired a semi-fixed 41lb High-Explosive (HE) round to a maximum distance of approximately 12,500 yards. (*Author's collection*)

A wartime drawing of a US Army 105mm howitzer M2A1 during the Italian campaign. The howitzer employed a percussion firing mechanism that activated a device on the cannon's breech to ignite the round's primer. The primer, in turn, ignited the round's propelling charge, pushing the projectile portion of the round from the cannon's barrel at a maximum muzzle velocity of 1,550 feet per second (fps). The howitzer's rate of fire ranged from two to four rounds per minute. (*US Army Center of Military History*)

(**Opposite, above**) Pictured here is a US Army 105mm M3 howitzer. The cannon was nothing more than a 105mm M2A1 howitzer barrel shortened by 27in. The M3 howitzer retained the breech mechanism of its larger cousin. Its carriage was a strengthened version of the carriage used for the M1A1 75mm pack howitzer. The maximum range of the 105mm M3 topped out at approximately 9,760 yards. The total weight of the barrel and carriage came to 2,159lb. (*National Archives*)

(**Opposite, below**) In a rush to build a self-propelled version of its 105mm howitzer M2A1, the army mounted the cannon in a semi-fixed forward-firing position on the M3 half-track. The mating of howitzer and half-track resulted in the vehicle pictured here, labeled the T19 HMC. The howitzer's traverse was 20 degrees left or right of the vehicle's centerline, with a maximum elevation of 35 degrees. A total of 324 examples of the expedient vehicle came off the production line. (*Patton Museum*)

(**Above**) The T19 HMC's replacement proved to be the fully-tracked 105mm howitzer M7 HMC, and an improved model the M7B1 HMC. The former was based on the M3 Medium Tank series chassis, whereas the latter was based on the M4A3 Medium Tank, with an example seen here in this wartime image. The 105mm howitzer with both versions traversed 30 degrees to the right and 15 degrees to the left. The maximum elevation came to 35 degrees on both models. (*National Archives*)

(**Opposite, above**) This photograph is of a preserved example of an M4A3 (105mm howitzer). There was also another version based on the M4 Medium Tank, designated the M4 (105mm howitzer). The 105mm howitzers in both vehicles bore the designation of the M4 and were fitted into the Combination Gun Mount M52. A total of 1,641 examples of the M4 105mm (howitzer) left the factory floor and 3,039 examples of the M4A3 (105mm howitzer) were completed by the end of the Second World War. (*Pierre-Olivier Buan*)

(**Opposite, below**) The French-designed and built 155mm howitzer Model 1917A1 employed by the US Army during the First World War and its post-war American-built copy, labeled the 155mm howitzer Model 1918A1, were initially fitted with wooden wheels that rode on steel rims. For high-speed towing, many were fitted with pneumatic tires and high-speed wheel bearings, beginning in 1935. Those 155mm howitzers not 'high-speeded' left the United States as military aid, and were known as Lend-Lease. (*Pierre-Olivier Buan*)

(**Above**) The US Army Ordnance Department began work on a replacement for the army's First World War-era 155mm howitzers in 1939. That replacement, pictured here, proved to be the 155mm howitzer M1. It had both a longer barrel than its predecessor and a newly-designed carriage. Visible under the carriage is a firing jack (pedestal). It allowed raising of the cannon's two wheels, creating a three-point support system for the weapon, one being the firing jack and the other two points being the trails' spades. This resulted in improved stability for the howitzer and improved accuracy. (*Pierre-Olivier Buan*)

(**Opposite, above**) Pictured here is a preserved example of the 4.5in gun. It looks very similar to the 155mm howitzer M1 as they share the same carriage, but reflecting its label as a gun, the barrel is longer by about 3ft. The large spring (matched by another on the opposite side) is an equilibrator. They aid in overcoming the unbalanced weight of a large and heavy barrel by keeping the barrel in balance at all angles of elevation so that it may be easily elevated or depressed by the crew. (*Chris Hughes*)

(**Opposite, below**) A wartime drawing of a 155mm gun M1A1 (Long Tom) in the Pacific Theater of Operations. Note the barrel hurtling rearward upon recoil. The barrel sat on a cradle which housed the recoil, counter-recoil and recuperator cylinder, which in turn was mounted on the anti-friction trunnion bearings of the top carriage. The top carriage housed the elevating and traversing mechanisms. (*US Army Center for Military History*)

(**Opposite, above**) The extremely long barrel of the 155mm gun M1A1, at 21ft, is evident in this photograph of a preserved example. The combined weight of the weapon's barrel and carriage came out at approximately 30,000lb (15 tons). The standard HE round it fired weighed about 95lb and had a maximum range of around 26,000 yards (just under 15 miles). A total of 1,882 examples of the gun, the 'Long Tom', came off the production lines by the war's end. (*Chris Hughes*)

(**Opposite, below**) Until a sufficient number of 155mm gun M1A1s (Long Toms) reached the US Army's field artillery batteries deployed overseas, the First World War-era French-designed and built GPF 155mm gun and its American-built copy the M1918A1 remained in service until mid-1943. Some went onto surplus and heavily-modified M3 medium tanks as seen here, creating what became labeled as the 155mm Gun Motor Carriage (GMC) M12. (*Richard Hunnicutt*)

(**Above**) The 8in howitzer M1, as shown here, was envisioned from the start as a sister piece to the 155mm gun M1A1, both using the same carriage. Other than the shorter (by 4ft) and thicker barrel, the two artillery pieces looked almost identical from a distance. The howitzer fired a 200lb HE round out to a maximum range of almost 19,000 yards (about 11 miles). A new breech ring added to production examples resulted in the designation M2. In total, around 1,000 examples of the M1 and M2 entered American military service. (*Pierre-Olivier Buan*)

(**Opposite, above**) To provide improved off-road mobility for its towed field artillery during the Second World War, the US Army fielded several unarmored fully-tracked towing vehicles, known in military nomenclature as 'prime movers'. The smallest version turned out to be the vehicle pictured here, towing an M2A1 105mm howitzer, labeled the 13-Ton High-Speed Tractor M5. It used tracks from the M3 Light Tank and a modified suspension system. On level ground, it had a top towing speed of 35mph. (*Author's collection*)

(**Opposite, below**) In addition to the 13-Ton High-Speed Tractor M5, the US Army placed into service the 18-Ton High-Speed Tractor M4 pictured here. Like the M5, the M4 rode on a modified suspension system of the M3 Light Tank. The intended role was towing the army's 155mm gun M1A1 (Long Tom) and the 8in howitzer M1/M2. It could also pull the 90mm Anti-Aircraft Gun M1/M1A1. The vehicle had room in its rear cargo compartment to carry some ammunition. (*Richard and Barb Eshleman*)

(**Above**) The US Army did, on occasion, employ captured artillery pieces against their former owners if a sufficient amount of ammunition for those weapons proved available while there existed a shortage of ammunition for its own artillery pieces, something that did occur at times during the fighting in Western Europe. In this photograph, we see American artillerymen firing a captured German Army 105mm gun optimized for counter-battery fire. (*National Archives*)

(**Opposite, above**) The largest and heaviest artillery pieces used by the US Army during the Second World included the sole preserved example seen here of the 8in gun M1. The barrel had a length of 34ft and the gun on its carriage came in at approximately 70,000lb (35 tons), about the weight of a second-generation M4 series medium tank. Firing an HE round weighing 374lb, it could reach a maximum range of around 35,200 yards (20 miles). (*Chris Hughes*)

(**Above**) The 8in gun M1 had a howitzer counterpart, the 240mm howitzer M1 pictured here in Italy, which initially found itself fitted to the same carriage. Unfortunately, testing revealed that the carriage in use with the 8in gun M1 could not accommodate the extra 10 degrees of elevation required by the howitzer. With the issue quickly addressed, the howitzer went off to Italy, arriving in May 1944. The weapon had a maximum range of approximately 22,225 yards (about 12.5 miles), firing a 360lb HE round. (*National Archives*)

(**Opposite, below**) The great length of the barrels of the 8in gun M1 and the 240mm howitzer M1 prevented their transport in a single load. The carriages, therefore, traveled separately from the barrels, as seen in this picture of an M3 medium tank series armored recovery vehicle (ARV) converted into a prime mover, towing the barrel of an 8in gun M1. Once the barrels and carriages arrived on site, a crane truck combined the two separate components. (*Patton Museum*)

(**Above**) The US Army's awareness of the Soviet and German armies' employment of mobile rocket artillery led to developmental work to see if such weapons could be a valuable addition to the services' inventory. An early example of this work was the T34 rocket-launcher, nicknamed the 'Calliope', seen here mounted on a first-generation M4 series medium tank. It consisted of a large number of plastic launching tubes loaded with M8 4.5in HE rockets. (*Patton Museum*)

(**Opposite, above**) With the outbreak of the First World War and the new threat posed by aircraft, the US Army's senior leadership decided that the Coast Artillery Corps would take responsibility for all anti-aircraft weapons. One of those proved to be the Model 1916 75mm gun pictured here, which had been modified as an anti-aircraft gun and mounted on a truck. A total of fifty-one examples came off the factory floor. None saw combat during the conflict. (*National Archives*)

(**Opposite, below**) The US Army fielded the 3in anti-aircraft (AA) gun M3 seen here, beginning in 1927. The following year a new carriage for the weapon went into production, designated the M2. The M2 was a pedestal mounting nicknamed the 'spider mount'. It had four long outrigger legs over which a steel mesh platform covered as a working platform for the weapon's crew. For towing, the outrigger legs and the steel mesh platform folded up into a compact mass. (*Public domain*)

(**Opposite, above**) To effectively engage enemy aircraft at night (before the advent of radar), carbon arc searchlights, with an example shown here, were employed. The internal components of the searchlight, which included the lamp and mirror, were housed in a large drum made of aluminum alloy or sheet steel, consisting of front and rear sections joined to form a single unit. Four jacks, one at each corner of the searchlight's trailer, supported the equipment during use and provided a means for leveling the trailer when emplaced. (*National Archives*)

(**Opposite, below**) The searchlights typically found themselves located off to one side of an anti-aircraft battery, their movements directed by a three-person control team, as pictured here, located somewhere between 300 and 500ft from the searchlights. The angular displacement of the control station handwheels transmitted electrically to the searchlight transformed it into mechanical energy, causing a corresponding angular movement of the searchlight mounted on a turntable. (*National Archives*)

(**Above**) To assist the searchlight control teams in aiming their devices in the direction of approaching hostile aircraft, the US Army had since the First World War used different versions of sound detection equipment. In this photograph, it consisted of three large circular horns with a microphone fitted at their base. They funneled sound into the operator's ears to aid him in determining both azimuth and elevation of incoming aircraft. The sound detection devices had a maximum range of 20 miles on a calm night. (*National Archives*)

(**Above**) The US Army's wartime replacement for the interwar sound detection equipment is the SCR-268 radar unit pictured here. The word radar stands for Radio Detecting and Ranging. Radar units themselves are relatively complex pieces of electronic equipment that send out radio waves, receiving echoes when the beam reflects back from an object. The echoes convert into pips of light displayed on a cathode-ray tube in such a manner that an operator can determine the bearing and range. (*National Archives*)

(**Opposite, above**) Behind the sandbags is a towed van containing the crew and electronic heart of a US Army SCR-584 gun-laying radar unit. Unlike the broad unfocused beams generated by the SCR-268, which had a difficult time discriminating between aircraft flying close together, the narrow microwave beams sent out by the SCR-584 could automatically track an individual target and give precise range, azimuth and elevation data to a gun director, which aimed the guns of an anti-aircraft battery. (*National Archives*)

(**Opposite, below**) Pictured here is the crew of a US Army M2 Optical Height-Finder. It formed part of the fire-control system of the service's larger anti-aircraft gun batteries. The soldier standing in front of the device is the altitude-setter. The three soldiers behind the device include the elevation tracker on the far right, the stereoscopic observer in the center and the azimuth tracker on the far left of the photograph. (*National Archives*)

(**Above**) Due to the apparent limitations of the M2 Optical Height-Finder, the US Army would go on to field the SCR-547 Height-Finding radar unit pictured here. The appearance of the identical radar dishes led to its popular nickname, the 'Mickey Mouse'. Height-finding radars are three-coordinate systems. They are capable of discriminating between targets that are close together, and they are capable of measuring range, bearing and altitude. As with all radars, there are a number of factors that can affect its ability to detect and track aerial objects. From a US Navy manual is a passage describing a few of the factors: 'Atmospheric conditions will sometimes affect target detection. A moisture-laden cloud might appear to be an air contact on the scope … Rain squalls, storms, etc., may temporarily obscure actual air contacts … Target detection is made more difficult when the enemy is jamming our radar.' (*National Archives*)

(**Opposite**) All the information provided by the various sensors (optical and radar) of a large-caliber anti-aircraft gun battery went to the M9A1 director shown. A primitive analog computer with attached telescopes, it continuously provided the mathematical firing solution predicting the flight paths of aircraft and furnishing fuze settings for multiple guns. That information went to the various guns in a battery via dial settings that the individual gun crews matched. From a US Navy manual is a description of an analog computer: 'An analog computer represents mathematical relationships by analogous mechanical motions and positions. These may vary from moment to moment by large or small amounts, but the solution is produced continuously. Its output at any given instant measures the values at that instant of the two or more changing quantities in the problem it has been designed to solve.' (*National Archives*)

(**Above**) The idea for the 90mm gun M1A1 pictured here had first appeared in 1936. The selection of that caliber was determined by the weight of a shell that could be hand-loaded; anything more than 40lb for a complete round would be too heavy for gun crews to load for more than a few minutes. The design consideration had been imposed on the army because a reliable mechanical loader did not yet exist. (*Public domain*)

(**Opposite, above**) The US Army's desire for a 120mm anti-aircraft gun dated back to the First World War. A prototype tested in October 1918 did not meet expectations. Developmental work on the weapon continued until 1921 when work on the project ended. With the start of the Second World War and a realization that bombing altitudes had increased to 30,000ft, the army once again began work on fielding a 120mm anti-aircraft gun. The eventual result was the fielding in 1940 of the 120mm gun M1 seen here. (*Chris Hughes*)

(**Opposite, below**) For towing the 120mm gun M1, weighing over 60,000lb (30 tons), and other large and heavy cannons, in 1943 the US Army fielded the 38-ton High-Speed Tractor M6 pictured here. Besides towing artillery pieces, it had room for their gun crews, ammunition (twenty-four rounds for the 120mm gun M1), and various other accessories. The M6 rode on the suspension system of the M3 light tank series. (*Pierre-Olivier Buan*)

(**Above**) The pilot Half-Track Multiple Gun Motor Carriage (MGMC) T28 had as armament a single 37mm automatic cannon and two .50 caliber water-cooled machine guns. However, it did not go into production. When a requirement arose for a vehicle that could engage both lightly-armored vehicles and aircraft, a slightly modified version of the MGMC T28 appeared as pictured here. It received the designation T28E1, was rushed into production and saw combat in North Africa. (*TACOM*)

(**Opposite, above**) It became evident to the US Army, with the successful German military invasions of Poland in 1939 and France in 1940, that the latter placed heavy reliance on ground-attack aircraft. The US Army, therefore, decided that it required a large number of fast-firing (automatic) short-range anti-aircraft weapons to defend its ground forces. One of the first examples of that need proved to be the Multiple Gun Motor Carriage (MGMC) M13, armed with two air-cooled .50 caliber machine guns. (*TACOM*)

(**Opposite, below**) Following in the developmental path of the Multiple Gun Motor Carriage (MGMC) M13, there eventually appeared the Multiple Gun Motor Carriage (MGMC) M16 pictured here. It came armed with four air-cooled .50 caliber machine guns. Production of the vehicle began in May 1943 and continued until the end of 1944, with some 3,618 examples completed. Many were conversions of M13s, upgraded to have two additional machine guns. (*Author's collection*)

RA PD 18534

(**Opposite, above**) Following the First World War, the US Army began thinking about the need for a 37mm anti-aircraft gun to fill the gap between short-range machine guns and the larger anti-aircraft guns designed to engage low-flying aircraft. The eventual result in 1938 would be the fielding of the 37mm anti-aircraft gun M1A2 shown here. Unfortunately, the weapon had some design shortcomings, which included an American-designed and built optical sighting system. (*National Archives*)

(**Opposite, below**) Unable to overcome many design issues with the 37mm anti-aircraft gun M1A2, the US Army began thinking about a replacement weapon. Fortunately, at the same time, a far superior gun of approximately the same size and caliber appeared on the scene. That weapon was a 40mm anti-aircraft gun designed by the Swedish firm of Bofors. The US Army quickly adopted the weapon seen here and assigned it the designation of the 40mm automatic gun M1. (*National Archives*)

(**Above**) To improve mobility of the 40mm automatic gun M1, the US Army initially experimented with mounting it on an M3 armored half-track. That didn't work as the gun and its supporting equipment badly overloaded the vehicle. The army then tried mounting an armored turret with the 40mm gun, as seen here, on the hull of an M4 series medium tank. That also proved unsatisfactory and was soon dropped. (*Patton Museum*)

(**Opposite, above**) Two coast artillerymen strain to close the breechblock (metal plug) of a cannon. The breechblock in this photograph is of the slotted-screw or interrupted-screw type with the DeBange obturator system. Some of the advantages of such a system appear in a US Army manual: '... strength, rapidity of operation, reduction of weight in the breech section ... uniform distribution of longitudinal stress produced by powder pressure developed in firing.' (*Public domain*)

(**Opposite, below**) A coast artilleryman is pictured loading the propellant charge into a 6in gun M1905A2. From an October 1944 manual is a description of the cannon: 'The 6-inch gun is a manually-loaded rapid-fire gun and has a maximum range of approximately 27,500 yards. It fires separately loaded ammunition and is directed by the data transmission system. An electric-hydraulic power unit, manually controlled, is used to elevate and depress the gun.' (*Public domain*)

(**Above**) The most impressive Coast Artillery Corps cannon in service during the Second World War would be the 16in gun Mark II, Model I pictured here on its barbette carriage. To protect it from enemy aircraft, it has been casemated in a concrete enclosure and covered by a thick layer of earth. The armored shield on the front of the weapon had a thickness of 4in and a sidewall 12ft high. (*Public domain*)

Chapter Five

The Cold War

Following the Second World War, as with all its major wars, the US Army became a shadow of its former self. From a wartime high of ninety-two divisions, by early 1950 that had dropped to just ten divisions, with only one at full strength. The Marine Corps went from a wartime strength of six divisions to less than one division by early 1950. The majority of artillery-men went home after the Second World War, with the bulk of the wartime-built artillery pieces going into storage.

In the immediate aftermath of the Second World War, US Army field artillery officers looked at lessons learned during the conflict and made recommendations. These included making all artillery self-propelled and increasing the number of 155mm howitzers at the division level so that infantry and armored divisions would not have to be so dependent on corps artillery support.

Atomic Cannon

Another primary concern of the US Army as a whole, and the field artillery branch in particular, was the impact that tactical atomic (nuclear) bombs would have on future battlefields. The army began giving more thought to how to incorporate atomic shells into its inventory of tubed field artillery.

Due to the size of nuclear warheads at that time, it would require an artillery piece with a caliber of at least 280mm. A cannon of such size was therefore approved for production in July 1951, at the start of the Korean War. Designated the M65 Motorized Heavy Gun, its popular but unofficial nicknames included the 'Atomic Cannon' and 'Atomic Annie'. It would be deployed in both the Far East (South Korea and Japan) as well as in Western Europe. However, it arrived in South Korea too late for the Korean War.

The towed gun depended on two tractor trucks for transport, one at either end. The total length of the two trucks and gun came out at 84ft with a width of 16ft. Weight was 168,000lb (84 tons). Once emplaced, which took fifteen minutes, the 100,000lb (50-ton weapon) could fire either a 900lb nuclear or conventional round.

A summary of the Atomic Cannon's relative effectiveness appears in the following passage from a US Army publication titled *King of Battle: A Branch History of the US Army's Field Artillery* by Boyd L. Dastrup:

> The gun was difficult to move and had a range of only 35,000 yards [17 miles] that fell short of the anticipated 45,000 to 49,000 yards [28 miles]. In view of the limited range, the piece had to be positioned too near the front to hit worthwhile targets and would be vulnerable to hostile action and require extensive protection.

The only time any of the Atomic Cannons fired a nuclear-armed round took place at the Nevada Test Site on May 25, 1953 with the initial production weapon. The twenty Atomic cannons built remained in service with the army until 1963 when nuclear warheads became small enough to fire from the existing 155mm howitzer and 8in howitzer. Also the army's fielding nuclear-armed guided missiles and rockets from much smaller and far less costly platforms made the Atomic Cannons unnecessary.

Honest John and Little John

An affordable and much more straightforward system was the MGR-1, named the 'Honest John'. It aimed at delivering tactical nuclear warheads, replacing the Atomic Cannon and entering service in 1953. The system consisted of a 6 × 6 truck fitted with a launch rail arrangement that fired a 27ft 3in, 5,280lb unguided rocket, armed either with a nuclear or conventional warhead.

The maximum range started at approximately 15 miles for the Honest John rocket, later upped to almost 30 miles with an improved version of the rocket. The later rocket design could also deliver chemical weapons. The Honest John remained in front-line US Army service until 1973 and in the US Army National Guard until 1983.

For the US Army's two post-war airborne divisions, there appeared in 1961 the MGR-3A, nicknamed the 'Little John'. It was a much smaller and more compact version of the Honest John rocket that was 14.5ft in length, weighed 780lb and had a range of approximately 12 miles. Like the Honest John, the Little John rocket carried either a conventional or nuclear-armed warhead. The Little John lasted in service until 1969.

Corporal and Sergeant

To supplement the Honest John was a radio-controlled guided missile, the MGM-5, nicknamed the 'Corporal', which entered service in 1954. The missile could be armed with either a conventional or nuclear warhead and had a range of around 120 miles. As the first nuclear-armed guided missile, Corporal had countless design problems that led to its replacement in 1964.

An example of the Corporal's poor reputation appears in the following extract from an April 1961 US Army report by the Army Ballistic Missile Agency: 'As to Army users, as testified by those who deployed with Corporal, Army personnel experienced keen resentment at playing the role of "guinea pigs" trying to learn how to control the erratic, temperamental, unpredictable Corporal – also a "guinea pig".'

The lessons learned from the failures of Corporal resulted in the fielding of the inertially-guided MGM-29 nicknamed the 'Sergeant'. The missile was 36ft in length, weighed around 10,000lb, had either a conventional or nuclear warhead and had a maximum effective range of around 75 miles.

Developmental work on the Sergeant began in 1955 and unfortunately, like its predecessor, endless design issues delayed its fielding until 1962. The Sergeant lasted in service until 1977. From a passage published in the April 1963 issue of *Artillery Trends* magazine is a description of the Sergeant's troubled development:

> The early submission of Sergeant requirements pushed missile 'state of the art' to its maximum limits. The Sergeant designers faced difficulties similar to those faced by a caveman trying to select a club. Should the 'club' be heavy and powerful or light and easy to carry? The requirements of air transportability, automatic checkout, simplicity of operation, ruggedness, reliability, etc., for the Sergeant were not always mutually compatible.

Lacrosse

Falling into the category of abject design failures was the MGM-18, officially nicknamed the 'Lacrosse'. Initially a Marine Corps requested item, the US Navy began work on the missile in 1947. In 1950, the project went to the US Army for further development. Endless design issues pushed the actual fielding of the weapon back until 1959.

The roughly 19ft long, radio-guided Lacrosse missile weighed 2,300lb and was launched from a modified 6 × 6 truck. With a maximum range of around 12 miles, it could carry either a 540lb conventional or nuclear warhead. Its intended role was to act as corps artillery, yet possess enough mobility to serve in the role of medium artillery.

As initially intended by the Marine Corps, they wanted an onboard electronic countermeasure (ECM) suite to protect the radio-guided Lacrosse from enemy jamming while in flight. Due to its cost, the army decided to do without that feature on the production examples. With that decision, the Marine Corps immediately dropped out of the program as they believed it was the one feature that would have made the Lacrosse a reliable and useful weapon.

Despite the Marine Corps' decision and a host of unresolved design and technical issues, the army justified ordering the Lacrosse into production based on '... operational requirements, atomic stockpile planning, an analysis of Soviet tactical doctrine, timeliness of availability to [the] troops, world situation, investment of over 200 million, other considerations.' These reasons came to naught in 1963, when the army realized the Lacrosse would never work and pulled all from service.

Redstone and Pershing

Based on captured German V-2 rocket technology, transported to the US and employing German wartime rocket engineers such as Werhner von Braun, the US Army placed the PGM-11 missile, officially nicknamed 'Redstone' into service in 1958. The inertially-guided missile had a length of 70ft, weighed 61,000lb and had a maximum range of approximately 200 miles. It could carry either a conventional or nuclear warhead.

The MGM-31A, officially nicknamed the 'Pershing', replaced the Redstone in 1964. A more advanced nuclear-armed missile using inertial guidance, it proved to be a great deal smaller and lighter than its predecessor. The 34ft-long missile weighed 10,000lb and greatly increased range over the Redstone. The Pershing flew to its target at Mach 8 (6,139mph).

The Pershing went through several iterations: Pershing 1, Pershing 1a and finally the Pershing II. From the February 1972 issue of *The Field Artilleryman* is this passage regarding the Pershing 1a: 'In its quick reaction alert role, Pershing takes its place alongside the Navy's Polaris and the Air Force's Minuteman and Titan systems as a deterrent against aggression. In this capacity the Pershing units in Europe are assigned strategic targets upon which to maintain continuous coverage.'

The army claimed that the Pershing II proved ten times more accurate than its predecessors and had a range of 1,118 miles. The Pershing series left service in 1991 under nuclear disarmament treaty obligations.

Lance

As a replacement for the Honest John and the Sergeant the army fielded the MGM-52, officially nicknamed the 'Lance', in 1972. Like the Sergeant, it had an inertial guidance system. Launched from a modified version of the fully-tracked M113 armored personnel carrier series, the 20ft-long, roughly 3,000lb missile had a maximum range of around 75 miles. The missile traveled to its target at a speed of Mach 3 or around 2,000mph. The Lance left service in 1991 under nuclear disarmament treaty obligations.

From the Redstone Arsenal website is a passage describing the intended role performed by the Lance: 'The LANCE's primary mission targets included enemy missile firing positions, airfields, transportation centers, command and logistics installations, critical terrain features (defiles, bridgeheads, main supply routes, etc.), and large troop concentrations.'

Davy Crockett

In 1958, the US Army began development of what eventually became the 'Davy Crockett' Battlefield Missile, XM-28/29. It consisted of a nuclear-armed 51lb spigot round for the M28 (120mm) Recoilless Rifle (that weighed 185lb and fired from a simple tripod) or the 440lb vehicle-mounted 155mm M29 Recoilless Rifle.

The Davy Crockett became operational in 1961 and remained in service until 1971. Due to its short range, its use in battle would have been as dangerous to the three-man crew as it would have been to the enemy. The army, therefore, suggested to the firing crews that they select firing positions in a sheltered location such as on the rear slopes of hills.

Still Useful

Wartime artillery pieces retained by the US military post-war included the towed 105mm M2A1 Howitzer, re-designated the M101A1, and the 155mm Howitzer M1, which became the M114 series post-war. The 155mm Gun M1, Long Tom, became the M59, and the 8in howitzer the M115.

All four weapons saw service in the Korean War. The least effective proved to be the Long Tom due to severe ammunition shortages, which would also affect the other artillery pieces in use during the conflict to varying degrees. Another serious problem throughout the conflict was the lack of trained artillery personnel, which meant that even if more cannons had arrived in theater, there were not enough artillerymen to man them.

The first six months of the Korean War proved a serious embarrassment to the army as a number of field artillery units were overrun by the North Korean Army with the loss of most of their equipment. In an answer to the poor showing by the field artillery in Korea, US Army General Matthew B. Ridgway would state in the fall of 1951 his take on the usefulness of field artillery in the fighting in Korea up to that time:

Whatever may have been the impression of our operations in Korea to date, artillery has been and remains the great killer of Communists. It remains the great saver of soldiers, American and Allied. There is a direct relation between the piles of shells in the ammunition supply points and the piles of corpses in the graves-registration collection points. The bigger the former, the smaller the latter, and vice versa.

The largest towed artillery pieces kept in the American military inventory long enough to see service during the Korean War proved to be the 240mm Howitzer M1. A dozen were brought out of storage and deployed to South Korea during the last three months of the war as there was then a plentiful supply of ammunition for the weapon. With the exhaustion of the weapon's ammunition stocks it left service in the late 1950s.

The Post-War Towed Replacements

As the M101A1 and the M114 series began aging out of the US Army artillery inventory, their eventual replacements showed up in service. Unhappy with the weight and size of the M101A1, the army fielded a lighter and more compact 105mm howitzer designated the M102. The first examples went to South Vietnam in 1966. The M102 fired a rocket-assisted projectile (RAP) to a maximum range of approximately 9 miles.

Beginning in 1989 the M102 was superseded by the towed 105mm howitzer M119 with the army. A license-built near-copy of the British-designed L118 Light Gun that entered service with the British Army in 1976, the M119's range, firing an RAP, went out to around 12 miles. The Marine Corps chose not to adopt either the M102 or M119 series and retained the M101A1.

From an online US Army fact file is the following description of the American version of the M119 and its capabilities:

Light enough to be airlifted and dropped, the M119 was designed to either be carried with slings by helicopter or dropped from transport aircraft. Its ability to be carried and packed so easily has made it one of the most versatile weapon systems in the US Army inventory, one reason the M119 remains in service today.

The replacement for the 155mm Howitzer M114 series in both US Army and Marine Corps' service was the towed 155mm M198 Howitzer, beginning in 1982. Its most important feature at the time was the approximately 18-mile maximum effective range with an RAP projectile. In addition to its increased range, the M198 could use all the stockpiled 155mm howitzer ammunition made for the M114 series.

Self-Propelled Artillery Too Late for the War

Some wartime developmental programs aimed at providing the army's artillery pieces with self-propelled (SP) mounts came off the factory floor

New Issue and the Solution

In the war in Europe, field artillery fought a linear war in which there was a fairly clear boundary between combatants. Field artillery proved unprepared at first for the type of warfare practiced by the enemy in Korea and later the Vietnam War, even though non-linear warfare had also occurred fighting the Japanese in the Pacific Theater of Operations.

A passage from an article titled 'Defense of the Artillery Battery' by Captain F.H. Hemphill, which appeared in the January 1967 issue of *Artillery Trends*, highlights some of the problems encountered by artillerymen during the Vietnam War:

> The demoralizingly effective firepower of artillery operating in a guerrilla environment coupled with the guerrilla's relative freedom of movement makes artillery batteries prime targets for guerrilla attacks. Such attacks may range from unsupported attempts at sabotage through infiltration attacks, either unsupported or supported by indirect fire, to full-scale attacks in force, supported by mortars, light artillery, recoilless rifles and other weapons.

Therefore, both Army and Marine Corps' fire support bases (FSBs) immediately set up 360-degree perimeters around their sites, protected by barbed wire, mines and machine-gun emplacements. Often an infantry company would be assigned to help in defending an FSB, as were self-propelled AAA guns. An explanation of an FSB comes from a US Army website:

> An FSB was built for one main purpose: to provide a base for field artillery to fire in support of infantry missions. Bases also fired to protect neighboring firebases, convoys traveling through their sector, and sometimes to simply fire 'Harassment and Interdiction' missions into the jungle where the enemy operated. The bases dotted the Vietnamese countryside, located strategically on hilltops and around pre-existing structures or airstrips to give maximum range and 360-degree coverage by the big guns.

too late to see combat during the Second World War. One of these was the 105mm HMC M37 based on components of the M24 Light Tank.

Production of the M37 had begun in January 1945. However, the end of the war resulted in only 150 examples rolling off the factory floor before the army canceled the contract. Those vehicles built, however, saw productive use during the Korean War (1950–53) alongside its predecessor, the self-propelled 105mm HMC M7.

Another cannon mounted on a fully-tracked chassis using components of the M24 Light Tank was the 155mm HMC M41. The Field Artillery Board recommended its standardization in June 1945. However, only eighty-five examples had come off the factory floor when the army canceled the contract. Like the 105mm HMC M37, the 155mm HMC M41 would go on to see service during the Korean War.

Additional Late-War SP Artillery

The M12 Second World War success resulted in the AGF requesting more of them. The problem was a lack of additional First World War-era 155mm gun barrels and the fact that the Long Tom's weight and recoil proved too much for the modified M3 medium tank chassis. Instead, Long Tom barrels went onto a new specially-designed fully-tracked universal chassis, which consisted of second-generation M4 series medium tank components.

The combination of the Long Tom barrel with the new fully-tracked chassis became the 155mm Gun M40. Production commenced in February 1945, with 418 examples completed. Tests of the 8in howitzer M1 on the new fully-tracked chassis also proved successful, leading to standardization of the combination as the 8in HMC M43 in November 1945. Both vehicles would go on to see combat during the Korean War.

The First Turreted SP Artillery

Anticipating the replacement of the M4 series of medium tanks, the AGF got together with the Ordnance Department in July 1946 to consider the next generation of self-propelled mounts for its new lighter-weight 155mm gun and an 8in howitzer. The army wanted both cannons to share the same weapon mount.

Instead of using a tank chassis, the army went with a specially-designed, fully-tracked chassis that featured a limited-traverse turret. That turret could accept both the 155mm gun and 8in howitzer. With the gun, the vehicle became the 155mm Self-Propelled Gun M53, and with the howitzer it became the 8in Self-Propelled Howitzer M55.

To maintain a certain degree of interchangeability between its fully-tracked vehicles, the self-propelled mount for the two cannons used the running gear and track from the early Patton Medium Tank series (M46 and M47) as well as power packs. Eventually, components from the M48 Medium Tank went into the specialized vehicle.

In 1956, the army decided it only required the 8in Self-Propelled Howitzer M55 and had all its 155mm Self-Propelled Guns M53 rebuilt to that configuration. The Marine Corps, however, decided to keep both the M53 and M55. The former would remain in service up through the Vietnam War before a new self-propelled howitzer arrived in theater.

A 170mm SP Gun

In 1950, the US Army identified a requirement for a self-propelled 170mm gun as a replacement for the 155mm gun on the M53. It intended that it go onto an upgraded version of the same vehicle used with the M53 and M55.

Three pilots, labeled the T162, were built and tested; however, at the same time, the army had become interested in lightweight fully-tracked platforms for its artillery that would be air-transportable. The T162 proved too heavy and oversized for transport by existing and proposed aircraft.

More Turreted SP Artillery

With the planned replacement of the wartime-developed M24 Light Tank, the army had to begin thinking about a substitute vehicle upon which to mount its existing 105mm howitzer. It also had to consider a new 155mm howitzer platform. A recommendation came for a self-propelled artillery piece featuring overhead armor protection from air-bursts. The platform eventually chosen for that role would be the new M41 Light Tank.

The heavily-modified chassis of that new light tank resulted in the 105mm Self-Propelled Howitzer M52 and the 155mm Self-Propelled Howitzer M44. Both vehicles had limited traverse armored turrets. A problem quickly arose concerning the M44 turret's poor ventilation. This led to a redesign of the vehicle which made it open-topped. A total of 648 examples of the M52 and 250 examples of the M44 came off the factory floor.

Despite the rush to place the M52 and the M44 in service for the Korean War, neither saw action before the conflict concluded. The rush into production resulted in numerous design issues with both vehicles. With a new engine, they received the suffix A1 in their designations. Both would be out of service before the Vietnam War, with many transferred to other countries' armies under foreign military aid programs.

The M109 Series

In 1952 the US Army was starting to think about future self-propelled howitzers. The result was standardization and production of a specialized, fully-tracked, aluminum armored vehicle in two different versions, starting in 1962. These included the 105mm Self-Propelled Howitzer M108 and the 155mm Self-Propelled Howitzer M109.

Unlike the M52 and M44, originally designed with limited traverse turrets, the M108 and the near-identical M109 had turrets that could traverse 360 degrees. As the M109's firepower was so far superior to that of the M108, the army eventually ended the M108's production after around 350 had come off the assembly line.

In an article titled 'The M109' by Lieutenant Colonel Walter R. Davis published in the June 1964 issue of *Field Artillery Trends* is the following extract describing the vehicle's advantages over the M44:

> ... a road speed in excess of 35 miles per hour; and an emplacement time of less than three minutes. In addition, the M109 howitzer weighs approximately 11,500 pounds less than its predecessor, the M44, while retaining full armor. Traverse and elevation can be accomplished in seconds with its hydraulically-operated turret. These features, combined with the accuracy and nuclear capability of the M109, make it an unusually versatile general-purpose weapon.

The initial production run of the M109 encompassed 2,111 vehicles, with 150 going to the Marine Corps. Due to unanticipated army demands, M109 production was restarted in the early 1970s, with many going off to a long list of international customers.

Both the M108 and M109 both saw combat in limited numbers during the Vietnam War with the US Army and Marine Corps, mostly in static

---

Artillery Observation Aircraft

The post-war replacement for the L-4 in the artillery observation role proved to be the single-engined L-19 (later designated the O-1). Dubbed the 'Bird Dog', a total of 3,200 came off the assembly lines for both the US Army and Marine Corps and served from 1950 until 1974. The Bird Dog also performed as a liaison aircraft.

Next in line was the twin-engined OV-1, nicknamed the 'Mohawk', of which 380 rolled off the factory floor. It performed other roles besides acting as a platform for FOs (forward observers). These included the light aircraft strike role and the emergency resupply role. Appearing in both US Air Force and army service was the twin-engined O-2 dubbed the 'Skymaster', 513 examples of which entered service. The O-2 served between 1967 and 2010.

Eventually the army began supplementing prop-planes in the artillery observation role with helicopters during the Vietnam War. These included the O-6, nicknamed the 'Cayuse', and the OH-58, dubbed the 'Kiowa'. Only the Kiowa remained in army service post-Vietnam War. It went through a series of iterations, ending with the OH-58D, nicknamed the 'Kiowa Warrior', which entered army service in 1984 and remained in use until 2016.

positions, as both services preferred lighter towed artillery pieces that could be moved by helicopters.

Improving the Breed

During the 1970s and 1980s the M109 was progressively upgraded, which created a series of extra suffixes added to the designation. Hence there was the M109A1 through the M109A4 versions. The A1 version came with a new longer barrel and the ability to fire rocket-assisted projectiles (RAPs).

In 1975, the army ordered 833 examples of a new, upgraded model of the M109 series assigned the suffix A2, and the rebuilding of the M109A1 model that became the M109A3 version. The addition of Nuclear, Biological and Chemical (NBC) protection features to the A2 and A3 versions resulted in the M109A4 version.

The Marine Corps retired their fleet of M109 series vehicles in the early 1980s in favor of its towed 155mm howitzers. However, some Marine Corps towed 155mm howitzer battalions switched to M109s during the run-up to Operation DESERT STORM (ODS, 1991) as they were in the pre-positioned stockpile of equipment when they arrived in the Middle East.

Air-Portable SP Artillery

In the army's quest to have self-propelled heavy artillery pieces light enough to be air-transportable, there eventually appeared the 175mm Gun M107 and the 8in Howitzer M110. Both were mounted on the same chassis, which was constructed of high-strength steel alloy and 0.5in (25mm) of steel armor on the very front of the vehicle. Initially powered by a gasoline engine, it eventually received a diesel engine.

Production of both the M107 and M110 began in 1962. The cannons sat on an exposed rotating platform on the rear of the vehicles' chassis. They are limited to a traverse of 30 degrees left or right of the vehicles' front. Both would see service with the US Army and the Marine Corps during the Vietnam War. Firing a conventional 174lb projectile, the M107 had a maximum range of around 25 miles.

Subsequent improvements to the vehicle and its cannons resulted in the M107A1 version. The M110A1 and A2 versions featured a longer barrel and the ability to fire RAPs, out to approximately 19 miles. When firing conventional 200lb projectiles, the M110 series had a range of approximately 15 miles.

In 1981, all the remaining US Army M107s went through an upgrade program to convert them into the M110A2 configuration. Problems with bore erosion that required increased maintenance compared to the M110 series and the M107's inaccuracy at longer ranges led to the army's decision.

The M110 series was pulled from service by the US Army in the early 1990s as the service decided it did not require any cannons over 155mm due to the widespread advent of precision-guided projectiles and vastly-improved computer targeting systems. Other reasons included the fact that during Operation DESERT STORM in 1991, the M110 series could not keep up with the M1 Abrams tank series or the M2/M3 Bradley Fighting Vehicle (BFV) series. There was also the advent of a new and much more effective self-propelled rocket system. The M110 lasted in US Army National Guard service until 2004.

Artillery Forward Observer Vehicles

In 1975, a recommendation by the US Army Close Support Study Group proposed the development of an M113 series vehicle labeled the Fire Support Team Vehicle (FIST-V). Its role was to provide field artillery support to the army's fast-moving armored units, including cavalry and mechanized infantry formations.

Outwardly the vehicle would resemble the M901 Improved TOW Vehicle (to make it less conspicuous on the battlefield). However, the TOW missile-launching mechanism (nicknamed the 'Hammerhead') would contain a laser designator, night sight and a gyrocompass instead of anti-tank missiles. When standardized in 1987, it became the M981 FIST-V, with approximately 800 entering army service.

The combat debut of the FIST-V occurred during Operation DESERT STORM and was not a success. In an article on lessons learned in ODS that appeared in the August 1991 issue of *Field Artillery* magazine appeared this extract regarding the shortcomings of the FIST-V: 'We can't provide fire support if we can't keep up with the maneuver forces we support. The current FIST-V is too slow and requires too much time to operate its observation system. We could quickly develop a FIST-V by modifying Bradley fighting vehicles.'

Rockets

Tests conducted at Fort Sill in 1944 and 1945 convinced the army that multiple rocket-launchers could provide the field artillery a boost in the amount of firepower it could deliver on the battlefields of the future. As a result, there was a great deal of developmental work done up until 1948, resulting in the army fielding the towed forty-five-tube M91 155mm Multiple Rocket-Launcher firing a specially-developed M55 chemical warfare rocket.

However, the initial excitement regarding the contribution that multiple rocket-launchers could make to the field artillery began to wane as field artillery officers decided that tube artillery remained more reliable and accurate. A renewed interest in multiple rocket-launchers did not develop until the mid-1970s. That led to fielding of the self-propelled M270 Multiple-Tube Rocket System (MLRS) in 1982.

Multiple Launch Rocket System (MLRS) Description

The M270 consists of a launcher unit that sits in the rear cargo bay of an M933 Carrier Vehicle, a version of the M2/M3 Bradley Fighting Vehicle (BFV) series. By the time production of the MLRS was completed in 1995, the US Army and the US Army National Guard had more than 800 examples in service. Upgraded versions of the MLRS continue to see service with the army.

The large, box-like MLRS launcher contains two bays, each of which houses a pod containing six 227mm rockets. The pod raises and lowers with hydraulics. The rockets' flight trajectory, and by default the range, depends on the elevation of the launcher tubes when fired. As with all rockets, those fired from the MLRS are unguided in flight and hence labeled as dumb rounds.

The primary MLRS mission is counter-battery fire. Its secondary missions include suppression of enemy air defense systems as well as interdiction fire against a variety of targets such as exposed troops, unarmored equipment and command and control centers. In an article titled 'Multiple Launch Rocket System Tactics' by Captain Richard M. Bishop, published in the May–June 1985 issue of the *Field Artillery Journal*, is the following boxed extract on the weapon:

A New Aerial Threat

From the May 29, 1946 report titled 'The War Department Equipment Board' headed by US Army General Joseph W. Stilwell is the following passage showing that those concerned appreciated the fact that weapon technology developed during the Second World War had made air defense a much more pressing issue:

In the past, anti-aircraft artillery fulfilled its mission in defense against manned aircraft if the percentage of hostile craft destroyed in each raid was high enough to make the cost to the enemy prohibitive. In future wars, no single airplane or bomb-carrying missile should be permitted to penetrate the defenses of a vital area because of the possibility that it might be carrying an atomic bomb. It is imperative

Submunitions

Beginning in the 1960s, the US Army started to employ its first generation of Improved Conventional Munitions (ICMs). These were transport/cargo rounds containing varying numbers of submunitions (grenades), both anti-tank and anti-personnel. Later versions included anti-tank and anti-personnel mines. Submunitions and 'cluster munitions' are the same.

The transport rounds contain a time fuze that goes off just before the projectile strikes the ground, detonating a bursting charge which ejects the submunitions over the chosen target area. The submunition grenades can penetrate up to 4in of armor if they land on a vehicle.

If the submunitions (grenades) do not strike a vehicle as they descend, they explode into fragments on impact with the ground. Pieces from the steel body of the submunitions (grenades) have a kill radius of about 50ft against exposed personnel. The few Iraqi soldiers that survived an attack by these submunitions during Operation DESERT STORM in 1991 called it 'steel rain'.

The downside of grenade submunitions is their very high dud rate and no self-destruct mechanism, resulting in unintentional casualties among friendly military personnel and civilians when unaware that they are in an area where submunitions exist. The larger submunition mines had self-destruct mechanisms that would render the mine inert after a prescribed length of time.

In 2008, then Defense Secretary Robert Gates signed the new Department of Defense Cluster Munitions Policy. It required that after 2018, the United States would no longer use cluster munitions that result in more than 1 percent unexploded ordnance.

that the effectiveness of anti-aircraft equipment be increased until the ultimate obtainable is reached in both conventional and newly-conceived types.

Skysweeper

An ADA gun that entered service in response to a recommendation by the War Department Equipment Board was the 75mm Gun M51, officially nicknamed the 'Skysweeper'. Early post-war, the US Army would begin to depend on long-range ADA missiles to replace the wartime AAA guns.

Unlike the wartime-fielded AAA guns, which depended on separate radars and electro-mechanical (analog) computers, the Skysweeper combined all these elements into a single platform. The design allowed the gun's operators to spot, track and intercept low-flying, high-speed enemy aircraft on their own. The weapon entered service in the mid-1950s.

The Skysweeper's radar could detect targets flying at up to 700mph and at an altitude of 43,000ft at a range of approximately 23 miles. Unlike the manually-loaded AAA guns that preceded it, the Skysweeper had an automatic loader, which provided a forty-five-round per minute rate of fire. It fired only proximity-fuzed rounds.

Advances in jet aircraft technology quickly rendered the Skysweeper obsolete, even as it was entering service. From a US Army online fact file is the explanation:

> By 1953, the [USAF] F-100 Super Sabre produced speeds of 863 miles per hour, with subsequent aircraft achieving higher speeds. The 1959 Russian MiG-21 'Fishbed' was capable of speeds of 1,384 miles per hour. By the late 1950s, the Skysweeper had begun to be phased out, with all units deactivated by the early 1970s.

Nike Missiles

The longer-ranged and higher-altitude counterparts to the Skysweeper were the US Army radar-guided 'Nike Ajax' missile, introduced into service in 1953, and the 'Nike Hercules' missile, which began replacing the Ajax in 1958. Both were two-stage missiles that flew to their targets, i.e. manned enemy bombers, at supersonic speeds.

Nike Ajax depended on a conventional high-explosive (HE) warhead to destroy individual enemy bombers, while the nuclear-armed warhead of the Nike Hercules could destroy entire enemy bomber formations by exploding above them, with the resulting blast effect blowing wings off bombers within a specific area.

The Nike Ajax flew at a speed of Mach 2.25 (1,710mph), and had a range of 30 miles and an effective altitude of 70,000ft. The larger Nike Hercules, a much-improved version of the Nike Ajax missile, flew at Mach 3.65

(2,750mph), had a range of 90 miles and an effective ceiling of 100,000ft. The army closed its last Nike Hercules missile site in 1979.

End of the Line

As the threat from enemy bombers was replaced by that of intercontinental ballistic missiles (ICBMs), the last iteration of the Nike series of missiles began development in 1958: the 'Nike Zeus'. The Nike Zeus was a larger and much-improved version of the Nike Hercules.

In tests, the Nike Zeus reached speeds of Mach 4 (3,000mph) and above and had a range of approximately 260 miles. With a ceiling of 897,000ft, it could, in theory, engage satellites. Interservice rivalry, escalating costs and doubts about its effectiveness led to its cancelation in 1963.

Hawk

The replacement for the Skysweeper, at the low- to medium-altitude ranges, proved to be the Homing All-The-Way Killer (HAWK) anti-aircraft missile system, the development of which began in the 1950s. Entering service in the 1960s, the Hawk consisted of a single-axle towed trailer mounting a triple missile launcher and several supporting vehicles, including a command and control vehicle and radar vehicles.

The first Hawk missile had a length of 12ft 6in, weighed 1,295lb and contained a 120lb warhead with a proximity and contact fuze. Powered by a solid-fuel rocket motor, it had a supersonic speed of Mach 2.5 (about 1,900mph). The maximum effective slant range of the original Hawk missile labeled the 'Basic Hawk' came in at approximately 15 miles. The missile could engage targets up to an altitude of 36,000ft.

To utilize the latest technology and remain effective against newer generations of enemy aircraft, an upgraded version – the Improved Hawk – entered service in 1971. Slightly longer than the original Hawk, it contained a larger 163lb warhead. It also had an improved guidance system and a new, more powerful rocket motor. The maximum effective range of the Improved Hawk increased to a slant range of 25 miles. The final version of the Hawk would be the Phase III Product Improvement Program (PIP).

Patriot

The US Army began phasing out the Hawk in the early 1990s. After two failed attempts to find a replacement, the army settled on what eventually became the NIM M-104 Patriot. It first appeared in 1981, reaching full operational capacity in 1984. Firing batteries arrived in West Germany the following year. A description of the surface-to-air (SAM) missile comes from the constructor's website: 'Patriot is a long-range, high-altitude, all-weather system designed to defeat advanced threats, including aircraft, tactical ballistic missiles and cruise missiles. Combat-proven during Operation Desert Storm [1991], Patriot can simultaneously engage multiple targets under the most severe electronic countermeasure conditions.'

The Patriot mounts on a towed trailer consisting of a single trainable pod with four enclosed missiles. The missile warhead came in at 200lb. As with the Hawk, its command and control and radar systems are mounted or towed by other wheeled vehicles. It takes around an hour for a Patriot battery to arrive at its chosen location and be ready to engage targets. A trailer-mounted diesel-electric generator supplies electrical power.

The original Patriot SAM had a maximum range of around 43 miles and an effective ceiling of almost 80,000ft. Continually improved over the years, the Patriot's operational parameters have significantly increased its range and reported effectiveness. Supposedly, the current maximum

---

Doubters

Some studies doubted the Patriot's effectiveness in Operation DESERT STORM, as claimed by the army in 1991. An example of that appears in an April 1992 Government Accounting Office (GAO) report:

> Our review indicated in general that the Army and supporting contractors overcame significant obstacles to provide tactical missile defense in Saudi Arabia and Israel but that the Project Manager's assessment that Patriot was successful against 70 percent of the Iraqi Scuds was not supported ... For example, there were several instances in which Patriot operators reported destroying more Scud warheads than there were missiles launched.

A very vocal critic of the army's claims of success for the Patriot, Theodore Postal of the Massachusetts Institute of Technology (MIT), stated that his research 'indicate[d] that Patriot was a near-total failure in terms of its ability to destroy, damage or divert Scud warheads.' Yitzhak Rabin, Israeli Prime Minister and a high-ranking military officer, went on to state: 'The biggest disappointment of the war is reserved for the Patriot. It was excellent public relations, but its intercept rate was rather poor.'

The army felt that those who questioned the battlefield effectiveness of the Patriot in combat had not gotten their facts right and mounted a fierce public relations campaign aimed at proving the weapon's critics wrong. That the Patriot remained in service reaffirms the army's belief in its effectiveness, whatever its true capabilities.

range of one of its newer missile models is about 100 miles, traveling at over Mach 4.1 (around 3,000mph).

Self-Propelled AAA Vehicles

To seek out a more suitable self-propelled AAA gun rather than the existing examples, and one fitted onto armored half-tracks, the AGF approved a wartime request from the Anti-Aircraft Board to install a twin 40mm AAA gun on a modified and open-topped chassis of the wartime M24 Light Tank. The vehicle received the designation Twin 40mm GMC M19, with production beginning in April 1945. An improved version of the M19 series bore the designation M19A1.

The M19 series would not see action in the Second World War but would see service during the Korean War. As there proved to be little or no threat from enemy aircraft during daylight hours in Korea, the M19 series primarily served in the ground support role. This role was also served by the Second World War Multiple Gun Motor Carriage M16B1.

The Duster

The eventual replacement for the M19 would be the Twin 40mm Self-Propelled Gun M42, standardized in October 1953. An upgraded model received the designation M42A1. Based on the modified chassis of the post-war M41 Light Tank, the original plan envisioned a separate vehicle carrying a radar fire-control unit to direct the M42's fire. That radar vehicle, designated the T53, never materialized due to technology short-comings and cost.

In total, 3,700 examples of the M42 series, nicknamed the 'Duster', were built by 1960. The army experimented with a range-only radar to fit onto the M42, but that was not a success due to cost. The army concluded by the early 1960s that non-radar-directed ADA guns were of limited effective-ness. Most of the M42s, therefore, went to US Army National Guard units in 1963, except for two army firing battalions stationed in Panama.

The army reactivated two M42 battalions and sent them to South Vietnam in 1966. Rather than air defense, their primary job proved to be in the ground support role. Following the Vietnam War, the Dusters were passed back to the US Army National Guard, which began disposing of them soon after. Those not transferred to other armies as foreign military aid would end their careers on firing ranges as hard targets.

Vulcan and Chaparral

In the early 1950s, the army embarked on a program to develop a suitable self-propelled, radar-equipped ADA gun system. Whatever AAA weapon system was selected would ride on the M113 series of fully-tracked vehicles, which initially entered production in 1960. All were built of aluminum to keep the weight down to make them air-transportable.

After some false starts, the army chose what eventually would become the Vulcan Air Defense System, designated the 20mm Self-Propelled ADA Gun M163, and with some modifications the M163A1. Armament consisted of a radar-guided, six-barrel 20mm Gatling gun designated the M168, an adaptation of a US Air Force (USAF) aircraft cannon.

In March 1960, the army began looking at a modified M113 chassis fitted with a complete guided missile system. It would receive the name 'Mauler' from the surface-to-air missile (SAM) it carried. However, with the simpler and less complex (hence less costly) Chaparral Guided Missile System entering service in 1969, the army canceled the Mauler program.

The Chaparral consisted of an M113-based launcher unit, armed with four infrared surface-to-air guided missiles. The missiles themselves, copies of the Sidewinder air-to-air infrared-guided missile, first entered service with the US Navy in 1956 and the USAF in 1964. The Vulcan and Chaparral were intended to work together on the battlefield.

Not Keeping Pace

To keep them up to date, both the Vulcan and Chaparral would go through many upgrades during their service careers. Despite improvements, the army eventually felt they were both obsolete. From a passage in a government publication titled *Archie to SAM: A Short Operational History of Ground-Based Air Defense* by Kenneth P. Werrell is the reason why:

> By the beginning of the 1970s, the Army concluded that both the Vulcan and Chaparral had serious operational limitations, which greatly reduced their battlefield effectiveness. Army efforts to replace the Vulcan with a more advanced gun system ended in disaster. The Army's concern over the Vulcan centered on its short range, its slow reaction times and the absence of both crew protection and the ability to distinguish friend from foe. The success of the Soviet ZSU-23-4 23mm guns mounted on a tank chassis in the Middle East wars and the rising threat of Soviet helicopter gunships were additional factors.

DIVAD and Roland

The army, as mentioned, tried without success to develop different vehicles to replace the Vulcan and Chaparral. They were the Divisional Air Defense (DIVAD) gun system, also known as the 'M247 Sergeant York', and the XM975 Roland Air Defense Vehicle, a mobile SAM system.

The DIVAD, armed with two radar-guided 40mm ADA guns, rode on the chassis of M48A5 medium tanks, and the missile-armed Roland launcher units on the rear cargo-bed of 6×6 trucks, although it was originally envisioned that the Roland would have been mounted on an M109 series chassis. Why the army chose those platforms is puzzling (other than cost) as none would have been able to keep up with the M1 Abrams tank series or the M2/M3 BFV series on the field of battle, the same vehicles they were intended to protect.

Both weapon systems proved disappointing due to unresolved design issues and cost overruns, despite warnings by the Government Accounting Office (GAO) predicting just that if they were placed into production. Those warnings were not heeded until the army's leadership finally discovered that the GAO had been correct. The Secretary of Defense therefore canceled DIVAD in 1985 after fifty vehicles had been delivered. The Roland program was canceled in 1988, also with fifty vehicles having been completed.

ADATS

Another self-propelled ADA vehicle seriously considered for adoption by the army in the late 1980s had been labeled the Air Defense Anti-Tank System (ADATS). It consisted of an American-designed and built dual-purpose laser-guided missile system, originally adopted by the Canadian Army mounted on an M113 series chassis. The US Army tested the missile-launcher and radar system mounted on an M2/M3 BFV chassis.

Despite the hope that ADATS would be the answer to the army's air defense needs, that did not prove to be the case. Testing of the weapon system proved unimpressive and, with the end of the Cold War and a sharp drop in available funding, the army terminated the program.

The Avenger

To fill part of the gap left by the cancellation of Sergeant York and the Roland, in 1988 the US Army fielded a wheeled anti-aircraft vehicle based on the High Mobility Multipurpose Wheeled Vehicle (HMMWV) chassis, better known as the Humvee. That vehicle became the AN/TWQ-1 Avenger.

The weapon system consists of an electrically-driven, one-man, gyro-stabilized rotating turret, armed with four ready-to-fire infrared-guided, Stinger anti-aircraft missiles on the rear cargo bay of a Humvee. For engaging close-in aerial or ground targets, the Avenger has a single .50 caliber M2 Browning machine gun.

The man-portable version of the Stinger appeared in 1982, with both the US Army and Marine Corps. When the Stinger missile activates on the Avenger, it takes less than fifteen seconds to ready the missile for firing.

Aiming the Avenger is done either with the gunner's direct view or from a Forward-Looking Infrared (FLIR) system. There is also a laser range-finder on the vehicle. The Avenger's Stinger missiles can engage a target while on the move. The Avenger crew can also fire its missile from a remote-control device up to a distance of 55 yards from the vehicle.

In the immediate aftermath of the Second World War, all three services of the American armed forces – Army, Navy and Air Force (formed in 1947) – were vying for the limited funding then available. As all thought that any future world war would involve nuclear weapons, the respective services rushed into production various delivery means. The US Army's initial solution proved to be the M56 atomic cannon pictured here, with a range of 17 miles. Development began in 1949, with the cannon in service from 1955 to 1962. (*Chun-Lun Hsu*)

(**Opposite, above**) Due to the M56 atomic cannon's high cost and immense size, the US Army embarked upon development of a series of more cost-effective and smaller rockets able to carry nuclear warheads. The first proved to be the MGR-1 Honest John unguided rocket, pictured here on its wheeled transport vehicle. First tested in 1951, the rocket was re-designated the M31, entered service with the US Army in 1953 and remained in the inventory until 1973. The final iteration of the rocket had a range of 30 miles. (*Pierre-Olivier Buan*)

(**Opposite, below**) Looking for a more compact and mobile nuclear-armed rocket-launcher system for its airborne divisions, the US Army eventually fielded what became known as the MGR-3 Little John in 1963. Both the unguided rocket and launcher trailer could be transported by cargo aircraft and air-dropped by parachute to its objective. Helicopters could also move the weapon. The rocket had a maximum range of about 12 miles and remained in the US Army inventory until 1970. (*National Archives*)

(**Above**) With the Korean War (1950–53) raging, the US Army found itself in a rush to deploy a nuclear warhead-armed guided missile. The result proved to be the MGM-5 Corporal missile tested in 1952, but due to numerous design issues it was not fielded until 1955. At that point, the army had given up on the Corporal and began development of a more promising missile design labeled the MGM-29 Sergeant, seen here prepared for launching. Sergeant served from 1962 until 1979. (*National Archives*)

(**Right**) On display in New York City's Grand Central Train Station in 1957 is a mock-up of a PGM-11 Redstone missile. Based on the wartime German V-2 rocket and developed with the assistance of German rocket engineers, it was the US Army's first nuclear-armed ballistic missile, with a maximum range of approximately 200 miles. Transported by a convoy of vehicles in the field, the missile had an inertial guidance system and would serve with the army from 1958 to 1964. (*National Archives*)

(**Opposite, above**) The replacement for the PGM-11 Redstone missile would be the MGM-31A Pershing nuclear-armed ballistic missile. Development began in 1956, with the first test example fired in 1960. It entered army service in 1960 and progressed through a series of improved versions, ending with the Pershing II in 1983. In this photograph, the crew of the vehicle in the foreground, which carried the nuclear warhead, has attached it to the body of the missile, carried by the second vehicle. (*National Archives*)

(**Below**) The US Army's replacement for the Honest John and the Sergeant turned out to be the MGM-52 Lance nuclear-armed guided missile, transported by an unarmored version of the M113 series of vehicles, as pictured here. From a US Army website is the following description of the weapon's role on the battlefield: 'Designed to attack key enemy targets beyond the range of cannon artillery and to reinforce the fires of other artillery units ... It filled the US Army's need for a highly mobile, medium-range, fin-stabilized, all-weather, surface-to-surface missile weapon system.' (*TACOM*)

Seen here during the Vietnam War (1965–75) is a US Army 105mm howitzer M102, the replacement for the Second World War-era 105mm howitzer M2A1, which was re-designated the M101A1 post-war. The cannon's carriage and trail are made from welded aluminum to reduce weight. Development began in 1955, with prototype testing in 1962 and the army taking it into service in 1964. The maximum range was 7 miles with a conventional round and 10 miles with a rocket-assisted projectile (RAP). (*National Archives*)

The US Army replacement for the 105mm howitzer M102 would be the 105mm howitzer M119 series pictured here, which began entering service in 1989. Rather than an American-designed cannon, it is a modified British-designed cannon, built under license. As with most long-serving weapons, it has gone through a series of improvements, with each assigned a slightly different suffix designation from A1 through A3. With a rocket-assisted projectile (RAP), the M119 series has a maximum range of 12 miles. (*DOD*)

An emplaced Marine Corps 155mm howitzer M198 is pictured here. It came about as the replacement for the Second World War-era 155mm howitzer M1, re-designated the M114 post-war. The M198's development began in 1968, with production starting in 1978. Firing a rocket-assisted projectile (RAP), it has a maximum range of 18 miles. For a brief time, a well-trained crew can fire off four rounds per minute. However, the sustained rate of fire is typically two rounds per minute. (*DOD*)

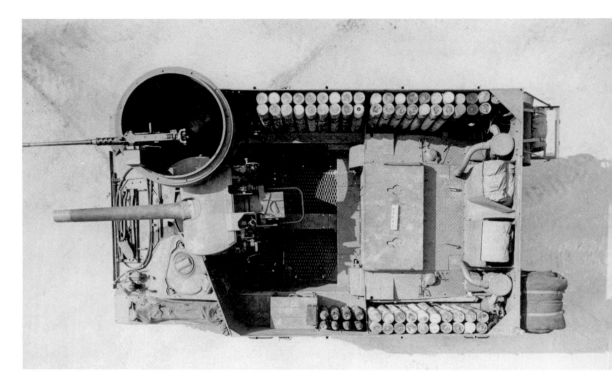

S/P How.
M 41
1944

(**Opposite, above**) The replacement for the M7 series, which had been based on the chassis of the M3 and M4 medium tank series, would be the M37 Howitzer Motor Carriage (HMC). It rode on a modified chassis of the M24 'Chaffee' light tank. Pictured here is a pilot model of the M37 designated the T65 with sixty-eight vertically-stored rounds of 105mm ammunition. The production version had its 105mm ammunition stored horizontally in bins to provide storage for 128 rounds. (*TACOM*)

(**Opposite, below**) A US Army program to develop a self-propelled 155mm howitzer based on either the Light Tank M7 (which never went into production) or the Light Tank M5 began in August 1941. Eventually the US Army decided that the M24 light tank chassis would be the best choice. The resulting vehicle, designated the 155mm HMC M41, is pictured here. Eighty-five examples came out of the factory before the conclusion of the Second World War, but none saw combat. They did, however, see service during the Korean War (1950–53). (*Christophe Vallier*)

(**Above**) With the success of the 155mm GMC M12, the US Army wanted more of the same. However, its inventory of interwar-era 155mm gun M1918 had been exhausted, and the existing M3 medium tank chassis could not handle the recoil generated by the recently-fielded 155mm gun M1. The army, therefore, came up with a new universal chassis based on second-generation suspension components upon which the 155mm gun M1 mounted. That combination became the 155mm GMC M40 pictured here. (*Patton Museum*)

(**Above**) The same universal chassis upon which the 155mm gun M1 found itself mounted also provided the platform for mounting an 8in howitzer. With that weapon fitted, the combination became the 8in M40 HMC, as shown here. Although a single pre-production example of each of the M40 and M43 made it to Western Europe before the German surrender, neither saw combat. Both the M40 and M43 saw combat during the Korean War (1950–53). (*Author's collection*)

(**Above**) With the impending invasion of Japan on its mind, the US Army began to develop self-propelled versions of the towed 240mm howitzer M1 and the 8in gun M1. The platform for both cannons was a lengthened version of the M26 Pershing heavy tank. Pictured here is the 8in gun T93 GMC, of which only two prototypes existed. Five of the 240mm howitzer-armed version referred to as the T92 HMC came off the factory floor. Both development programs were canceled following the conflict. (*Patton Museum*)

(**Opposite, below**) In the immediate post-war period, the US Army looked at replacing the 155mm GMC M40 and the 8in HMC M43 using a new fully-tracked universal chassis, based on components from the recently-introduced M47 Patton medium tank. Armed with the 155mm gun M1, the new chassis became the M53 GMC, and when armed with the 8in howitzer M2, it became the M55 HMC pictured here. The two types of cannon were interchangeable between vehicles. (*Christophe Vallier*)

(**Above**) In the early post-war period, the US Army concluded that overhead armor protection was an essential requirement for new self-propelled artillery pieces. As the M41 light tank was in the process of replacing the Second World War-era M24 light tank, it was the chassis of choice. Unable to resolve ventilation design issues, the army accepted into service the open-topped 155mm self-propelled howitzer M44 shown here, with an improved version becoming the M44A1. (*TACOM*)

(**Opposite, above**) The US Army had more success with the counterpart of the M44, also based on the M41 light tank chassis, seen here and designated the 105mm self-propelled howitzer M52. Production began in 1951, with a total of 684 examples coming off the factory floor. Re-engined, it received the designation of the M52A1. Armor thickness on the vehicle topped out at 13mm. The turret on the M55 series could only traverse 60 degrees right or left. (*Chris Hughes*)

(**Opposite, below**) In 1953, the US Army began thinking about a new fully-tracked universal chassis upon which to mount either a 105mm or 155mm howitzer. There existed two key design features required: aluminum alloy armor and a turret that traversed 360 degrees. Earlier self-propelled artillery turrets had only limited traverse. Production of the M108 pictured here, armed with the 105mm howitzer, began in 1962. It would see service during the Vietnam War. (*Chris Hughes*)

(**Above**) At the same time that production of the 105mm howitzer-armed M108 began, construction of its 155mm howitzer-armed counterpart also started. The latter received the designation M109, with an example pictured here. Within a year, it had become apparent that the M108 version made no sense, so production ended in 1963 with 350 examples completed. The M109 continued in production until 1969, with a total of 1,961 examples acquired by the army and another 150 by the US Marine Corps. (*TACOM*)

(**Opposite, above**) The M109 would see service during the Vietnam War (1965–75). When firing full-charge rounds to achieve maximum range, it was realized that the resulting blast effect proved physically hard on the crews and damaged the vehicles. A new longer-barreled 155mm howitzer, seen here, retrofitted to all M109s in the inventory, corrected the problem. The change to the vehicle resulted in the designation M109A1. (*Public domain*)

(**Opposite, below**) A continuous succession of improvements to the M109 series resulted in new suffixes added to its original designation. Newly-built vehicles such as the example pictured here received the designation M109A2. When earlier production vehicles such as the M109 and M109A1 were modernized, they received the designation M109A3. Later upgrades to the M10A3 inventory of vehicles resulted in their being re-designated the M109A4. With a new version of the 155mm howitzer added, they became M109A5s. (*Public domain*)

(**Above**) At different times, the US Army has seemed obsessed with the concept of lightness with its ground equipment. In 1955, there began a significant emphasis on fielding combat vehicles compact enough to be transportable by the US Air Force's existing cargo aircraft. Again, a universal chassis was developed that could mount either a 175mm gun or an 8in howitzer. The vehicle pictured here received the designation of the 175mm self-propelled gun M107. For transport by air, the cannon barrel retracted. (*TACOM*)

(**Opposite, above**) The counterpart to the US Army 175mm self-propelled gun M107 proved to be the 8in self-propelled howitzer M110 seen here in South Vietnam. The fully-tracked chassis on which both cannons were mounted consisted of welded high-strength alloy steel. Eventually powered by a diesel engine, the only armor on the vehicle consisted of 0.5in at the hull front and around the driver's position. Turret traverse for both cannons was either hydraulic or manual. (*TACOM*)

(**Below**) In 1987 the US Army began fielding the M981 Fire Support Team Vehicle (FIST-V) seen here to improve its artillery forward observers' mobility. Based on the M113 series of armored personnel carriers, the vehicle has a laser for determining the range to targets, as well as an inertial navigation system, radios and eventually the addition of GPS. The M981 looks almost identical to the M901 improved TOW to prevent the enemy singling it out for immediate destruction. (*TACOM*)

(**Above**) Following the Second World War, the US Army's wartime anti-aircraft guns were incapable of tracking and developing firing solutions for jet aircraft due to their higher speed. Their replacement for engaging enemy aircraft flying at intermediate altitudes up to 20,000ft proved to be the 75mm M51 anti-aircraft gun pictured here in its transport configuration. Due to advancements in the field of electronics, the M51 gun mount incorporated not just the gun and automatic loading mechanism, but an analog computer and radar. (*Richard and Barb Eshleman*)

(**Opposite, above**) Complementing the 75mm M51 anti-aircraft gun, the US Army fielded several anti-aircraft missiles for engaging enemy aircraft flying at higher altitudes. These included the Nike Ajax, introduced in 1953, its replacement the Nike Hercules pictured here, which entered service in 1958, and the Nike Zeus, the last of the Nike missile series. Zeus never entered into production as the army canceled it in 1963 in favor of a more advanced missile design. The Nike Hercules lasted in service until 1979. (*Public domain*)

(**Opposite, below**) With America's leading Cold War opponent, the Soviet Union, fielding ever-faster jet aircraft, the 75mm M51 anti-aircraft gun was withdrawn from US Army service by the late 1950s. As no anti-aircraft gun system could match the speed of the latest jet aircraft, the army began work on the immediate-range anti-aircraft missile seen here, labeled the Hawk (Homing All-the-Way Killer). It served with the American military from 1959 until 2002 in a series of progressively-improved versions. (*Public domain*)

(**Opposite, above**) The US Army's replacement for the Nike Hercules is the Patriot, which entered into service in 1990. The anti-aircraft missile system battery is brought onto the site by an assortment of wheeled vehicles. The missile comes in pods of four, in sealed containers, mounted on a semi-truck trailer as seen in this illustration. The large radar unit for each firing battery also rides on a semi-truck trailer. Continuously updated during its time in service, the army is expecting Patriot to remain a viable weapon system until 2040. (*US Army Center for Military History*)

(**Opposite, below**) The US Army's desire for a self-propelled 40mm anti-aircraft gun in the Second World War resulted in the 40mm MGMC M19 pictured here, armed with twin 40mm guns. Mounted on the lengthened chassis of the M24 light tank, production began in April 1945. A total of 300 examples came off the assembly lines before the army canceled the program in August 1945 following the Japanese surrender. No M19s saw combat in the Second World War, but did see use during the Korean War (1950–53) in the ground support role. (*Pierre-Olivier Buan*)

(**Above**) With the introduction of the post-war-developed M41 light tank, the US Army decided to take the M19's existing twin 40mm anti-aircraft gun mount and fit it onto a modified chassis of an M41. The combination received the designation M42 40mm self-propelled anti-aircraft gun. An attempt to provide the vehicle with a radar unit failed. The M42 saw combat during the Vietnam War, but only in a ground support role. (*TACOM*)

(**Above**) In 1952, the US Army began the development of a gun-based system that could deal with low-flying jet aircraft. After a couple of design dead ends, the army decided to adopt the M113 series-based vehicle labeled the M163 Vulcan Air Defense System (VADS), also referred to as a self-propelled anti-aircraft gun (SPAAG). Entering service at the same time was the towed version pictured here, designated the M167 Vulcan Air Defense System (VADS). (*Public domain*)

(**Opposite**) Complementing the Vulcan in protecting the US Army's forward ground forces from aerial attack was the MIM-72 Chaparral pictured here. Like the former, it rode on an M113 series vehicle chassis. The Chaparral missile is a version of the AIM-9 Sidewinder air-to-air missile, still employed by both US Navy and US Air Force fighters. Besides the four launch-rail-mounted missiles, the vehicle had storage space for eight additional missiles. (*Public domain*)

(**Above**) Pictured here is a US Army M270 Multiple Launch Rocket System (MLRS) unleashing one of its twelve onboard rockets. The concept for the weapon system began in the late 1970s, with the first vehicles entering army service in 1982. The two Launch Pod Containers (LPCs) fit onto the chassis of the M2/M3 Bradley family of vehicles. The rockets fired from the MLRS contain hundreds of submunitions. They disperse over a target at a pre-determined altitude and blanket an area with anti-personnel and anti-tank bomblets. (*TACOM*)

(**Opposite, above**) The US Army concluded in the 1970s that the M163 Vulcan Air Defense System (VADS) and the MIM-72 Chaparral were ineffective at protecting the service's armored formations from enemy aircraft and attack helicopters. What eventually evolved to replace them was the M247 Sergeant York Division Air Defense (DIVAD) in 1984, an illustration of which is shown here. Unresolved design issues led to its cancellation the following year, with fifty examples having entered service. (*Patton Museum*)

(**Opposite, below**) The failure of the M247 Sergeant York Division Air Defense (DIVAD) left the US Army still requiring a replacement for the M163 Vulcan Air Defense System (VADS) and the MIM-72 Chaparral. American industry developed an anti-aircraft weapon system consisting of a one-person powered turret armed with two pods, each containing four surface-to-air Stinger missiles, mounted on a Humvee as pictured here. The army liked what they saw and ordered the first 325 examples in 1987. (*DOD*)

Chapter Six

Post-Cold War

Paladin

The last version of the M109 series placed into development before the Cold War ended in 1991 eventually acquired the designation M109A6 and its official nickname of the 'Paladin'. Its development had begun in 1979. The first production example entered the army's inventory in 1993.

Instead of newly-built vehicles, the Paladin consisted of rebuilt M109A2 and A3 vehicle hulls, with the introduction of an entirely new and larger turret. The most noticeable external detail on the Paladin, when compared to earlier versions of the M109 series, is the large steel armored ammunition bustle attached to the rear of the vehicle's turret.

In the immediate post-war period, the US Army decided to reduce the number of Paladins in front-line service by replacing them with the more battlefield-effective M270 MLRS. Surplus Paladins went to the US Army National Guard, replacing the Guard's older-generation M109 series vehicles, a process that took until 2003 to complete.

Paladin in Operation

The brains of the Paladin consist of a fully-automatic fire-control system connected to an integrated inertial navigation system with an embedded Global Positioning System (GPS). These electronic devices allow the vehicle to receive a fire mission via digital radio and immediately compute all needed firing data while on the move. At the same time, the Paladin's onboard computers put together the firing data and direct the vehicle's driver to an optimal firing position.

Once at its chosen firing position, the onboard computer automatically unlocks the 155mm howitzer barrel from its travel lock, points the cannon in the direction of the target and fires the first round of ammunition. All of this takes place in just under a minute after the vehicle comes to a halt.

After completing a fire mission, the Paladin's gunner can fire four rounds per minute for about three minutes. The howitzer barrel then automatically returns to its travel lock and the vehicle can leave the site before the enemy can react with radar-directed counter-battery fire, which can arrive in mere minutes. By comparison, the M109A2 and M109A3 took eleven minutes to complete the same process.

In an after-action report compiled by the US Army 3rd Infantry Division concerning Operation IRAQI FREEDOM in 2003 appears the following extract: 'The combat performance of the M109A6 Paladin was magnificent. It is an extremely capable system that consistently put rounds downrange in less than two minutes after mission receipt, even while on the march.'

On the downside, the 3rd Infantry Division also discovered a serious shortcoming of the Paladin as appears in this passage in the July–August 2003 issue of *Field Artillery* magazine, in an article titled 'Observations from Iraq: The 3rd Division in OIF': 'Our final concern is that the Paladin was easily outranged by [some] Iraqi cannon systems ... This created force protection concerns.'

Smart Rounds

The 155mm howitzer on the Paladin can fire a variety of conventional and unconventional artillery rounds. Since conventional munitions have no mechanism to change course once in flight, they are called 'dumb rounds'. These would have included the rocket-assisted M549 RAP round with a range of 18 miles.

The army's first precision round intended for the Paladin was the M712. Known as a 'smart round', it was officially dubbed the 'Copperhead'. Its first test-firing took place in 1972. However, its short range and the inability to operate in the rain or fog resulted in its cancellation in the mid-1980s.

Another issue that had plagued the Copperhead was that it was not a 'fire-and-forget' weapon and depended on an observer in the air or on the ground to keep a laser designator pointed at the target during flight. That observer may be unable to maintain a lock on a target due to terrain, weather conditions or enemy countermeasures such as smoke or fire on their location.

Fewer than 100 Copperhead rounds were fired by the US Army during Operation DESERT STORM in 1991. Surviving Copperhead rounds remain in the army's inventory, with some going to Lebanon's Army which has employed them with great success in urban combat situations.

SADARM

The second precision round intended for the M109 was the M989 Sense and Destroy Armor (SADARM) submunition. Developed during the Cold War as a fire-and-forget weapon for dealing with large formations of Soviet Army tanks, it appeared in service use in 1995. From an October 2017 US Army press release: 'The SADARM projectile contains two

> ## EFP Effects
> In the July–August 2000 issue of *Field Artillery* magazine a description of what happens to an armored vehicle when struck by an EFP:
>
> A direct hit with the EFP often results in the complete destruction of the target vehicle. The EFP penetrates the vehicle with tremendous kinetic energy, striking critical components and causing mobility, firepower and catastrophic kills. Inside the vehicle, casualties also are caused by the 'spalling' effect of the EFP's penetration. The molten fragments of the vehicle's armor shell and the EFP set off powder increments, detonate on-board ammunition and ignite fuel.

sensor-fuzed munitions, which, after expulsion from the carrier, scan the ground during descent for armored vehicle targets. Upon detection, they fire an explosively-formed penetrator (EFP) through the target's roof, defeating the vehicle.'

Technical issues and the end of the Cold War resulted in the army canceling SADARM production in 2002 after approximately 1,000 rounds entered inventory. Some of the SADARMs saw use during Operation IRAQI FREEDOM.

In an article from the July–August 2003 issue of *Field Artillery* magazine is the following extract: 'SADARM was so effective that maneuver commanders asked to use it to destroy stationary vehicles rather than using massed artillery. The drawback to these munitions is its 2-kilometer [2,187 yards] danger close range and susceptibility to temperature inversions and restrictions during windy conditions.'

Excalibur

The Copperhead's and SADARM's replacement proved to be the much longer-ranged and more capable fire-and-forget M982 Extended Range Precision (ERAP) munition, officially nicknamed 'Excalibur', that entered into field use in 2005. A partial description of the Excalibur appears in a US Army online fact file: 'The Excalibur projectile uses a jam-resistant internal GPS receiver to update the inertial navigation system, providing precision in-flight guidance and dramatically improving accuracy to less than 2 meters [about 2 yards] miss distance regardless of range.'

From the July–August 2006 issue of *Field Artillery* magazine is a passage on the Excalibur's effectiveness: 'This munition can range to 40 kilometers [about 25 miles] and has a near-vertical trajectory for use in urban or close terrain operations or in close support of troops.'

The Pressure is On

As other major armies have switched to ever more advanced precision artillery rounds, the US Army has had to keep up. That effort is now one of the army's top priorities, labeled as the 'Long Range Precision Fires', which, according to the army, support its requirements 'for both close and deep-strike capabilities against a near-peer adversary.' During testing in 2019, the army's upgraded Excalibur round demonstrated an increase in range beyond 25 miles.

A new extended-range precision munition, with low-rate production slated to begin in 2022, is the XM1113, labeled as an Insensitive High-Explosive Rocket-Assisted Projectile. It is to replace the army's aging M549A1 155mm RAP round. Taken from an army online fact file:

> The XM1113 uses a large high-performance rocket motor that delivers nearly three times the amount of thrust when compared to the legacy M549A1 RAP. Its exterior profile shape has also been streamlined for lower drag to achieve the 40-plus kilometers [about 25 miles] when fired from the existing fielded 39-caliber 155mm weapon systems.

Improving Dumb Rounds

The army fielded the M1156 Precision Guidance Kit (PGK) in 2016 to upgrade the battlefield effectiveness of its existing stockpile of 155mm conventional rounds. The PGK contains a GPS guidance kit with fuze functions as well as an integrated GPS receiver to correct for errors associated with ballistic firing solutions, greatly reducing the number of artillery rounds required to destroy targets.

An article appearing in the January–February 2007 issue of *Field Artillery* magazine describes the intended targets for the new artillery round guidance kit:

> PGK will be considered an 'area precision munition', meaning it is an area-fired munition that is more precise than conventional rounds. Target sets are the same as for any HE projectile. Some targets may be better suited for use with PGK, such as linear targets (bridges, roads

and convoys, troops in the open, etc.) or high pay-off targets (HPTs), such as tactical operations centers (TOCs) and command posts (CPs).

The PGK is placed on the nose of an M795 or M549A1 HE projectile and is programmed with the target's GPS coordinates and guides itself to the location with an accuracy of less than 33 yards. Appearing in an April 2015 US Army press release is the following passage that explains a feature of the PGK that prevents after-battle casualties to friendly forces and civilians:

> PGK technology provides greater precision and lethality for American troops, but it also reduces the potential for collateral damage to friendly troops and non-combatants by incorporating a 'fail-safe' option, which prevents a PGK-equipped artillery round from detonating if it does not get close enough to the target location.

In anticipation of engaging in combat with an enemy capable of jamming its GPS-guided artillery rounds such as the PGK, the army began fielding a GPS jam-resistant version of the PGK labeled the PGK-Modernization round. It is also developing artillery rounds that will not require GPS. The current label for this new technology is Position, Navigation and Timing (PNT), which will provide GPS-like guidance, navigation and targeting, without actually requiring satellites.

Proposed Paladin Replacement

In 1984, the US Army envisioned a replacement for the Paladin, which eventually became the XM 2001, officially nicknamed the 'Crusader'. In 1997, the GAO suggested the army acquire an already-proven German-designed and built self-propelled 155m howitzer, an idea quickly rejected.

Unmanned Aerial Platforms

In the early 1970s, the army first began looking at remote-controlled, unmanned aircraft for performing the role of FO. These aerial platforms have gone by a number of labels over the decades, including drones, Remotely Piloted Vehicles (RPVs), Unmanned Aerial Vehicles (UAVs) and now Unmanned Aerial Systems (UASs).

The newest iteration, which entered service with the army in 2002 and is now employed by the Marine Corps, is the RQ-7 series nicknamed the 'Shadow'. A description of what it does appear in a 2018 Army publication: '. . . provides reconnaissance, surveillance, target acquisition and force protection for the Brigade Combat Team (BCT) in near-real-time during day, night and limited adverse weather conditions.'

In 1997 a GAO report stated that no existing 155mm self-propelled howitzer met all the requirements posed by the army for the Crusader.

By 2002, the army had set its sights on having 480 examples of the Crusader. That same year, however, the Secretary of Defense canceled the Crusader program for several reasons, including its costs and weight; the latter exceeded what could be carried safely by the USAF's existing transport aircraft. In the Secretary of Defense's May 2003 report to Congress, the reasoning behind the Crusader's cancellation was laid out:

> In short, the decision to recommend that we skip Crusader is one that emphasizes accelerating the shift to precision munitions of all indirect fire systems – cannon as well as rocket, Marine Corps, as well as Army ... In the near to mid-term, however, our conclusion is that accelerating precision rounds for indirect fire systems will increase the overall capability of our forces more than procuring 480 Crusader platforms.

Another Failure

In 2000, the army began looking at a lightweight family of fourteen tracked vehicles, both manned and unmanned, all using the same chassis, transportable by the C-130. That family of proposed vehicles fell under the heading of the Future Combat System (FCS). Within that heading, there appeared a 155mm self-propelled howitzer referred to as the XM1203 Non-Line-of-Sight Cannon (NLOS-C), with five prototypes built.

Due to ever-increasing costs and unforeseen delays due to pushing along immature technology, as well as a shift to fighting insurgencies rather than conventional wars, the Secretary of Defense canceled the program in 2009. His explanation was as follows:

> I have concluded that there are significant unanswered questions concerning the FCS vehicle design strategy. I am also concerned that, despite some adjustments, the FCS vehicles – where lower weight, higher fuel efficiency and greater informational awareness are expected to compensate for less armor – do not adequately reflect the lessons of counterinsurgency and close-quarter combat in Iraq and Afghanistan.

M109A7

With the cancellation of the Crusader and the NLOS-C and the need to keep its inventory of 155mm self-propelled howitzers up to date, a decision came about by the army to build upon the Paladin by introducing the M109A7 in 2019.

The M109A7 uses the existing main armament and turret of a Paladin and replaces the vehicle's hull with a new design using the mobility components from the latest version of the M2/M3 Bradley series. Some of the technology that went into the M109A7 came from the canceled NLOS-C.

Some new features have also been added to the M109A7 to improve its battlefield effectiveness, as seen in the following passage from an online US Army fact file: 'The platforms will also be fitted with Blue Force Tracker capability to ensure situational awareness with other friendly forces ... The new electric-gun drives and rammer components, as well as a microclimate air conditioning system, will be powered by the common modular power system.'

Upgrading the M270 MLRS

The M270 MLRS was beginning to show its age by the late 1990s. Most of its electronic hardware was no longer in production and the software had become obsolete. Another problem that became apparent during Operation DESERT STORM was the vehicle's slow reload time, a long-time problem common to all rocket artillery. Highly-mobile enemy formations could easily move to a new position during the time it took to reload the two six-round rocket pods. The army deployed the first of the new M270A1 MLRS vehicles in 2000 to address these problems.

The most significant improvement in the M270A1 MLRS upgrade was a new fire-control system. It was compatible with the then-current range of rockets and missiles and also had the growth potential to handle new models then under development for the M270A1 MLRS. Unlike the older fire-control system built on its operating system, the new system used Microsoft Windows as its software platform. A GPS-aided navigation system for the launcher supplemented the existing inertial position-navigation system.

The combination of improvements allowed the M270A1 MLRS crew to aim the launcher in just sixteen seconds. The M270 MLRS launcher had taken ninety-three seconds to accomplish the same feat. Reload time also improved thanks to a faster launcher drive system.

Based on a recommendation in 2017, the army went ahead with a program to upgrade the M270 MLRS series once again, resulting in the fielding of the M270A2 version of the vehicle. From a passage in an online army fact file is a description of what will take place:

The initiative will expand the MLRS fleet by up to 160 vehicles via conversion of obsolete, unserviceable M270A0 MLRS launchers during fiscal year 2019–2022. The program will also upgrade 225 current

> ## M270 MLRS Problems
> On the negative side, concerning the M270 MLRS series range and precision demonstrated in Operation IRAQI FREEDOM, V Corps leadership remarked in a 2003 after-action report inadequate range and accuracy 'do not allow for firing in the proximity of friendly troops or in areas of potential collateral damage. This unnecessarily makes close air support a more viable option for the maneuver commander.'
>
> In the September–October 2003 issue of *Field Artillery* magazine is an extract from an article titled 'The Sound of Thunder VCA in Operation Iraqi Freedom': 'The range of the M26 [rocket] also placed M270 units at a disadvantage when encountering enemy long-range artillery.'

M270A1 MLRS launchers during fiscal year 2022–2030. This fleet expansion will modernize the vehicles to extend the operational life through 2050.

Increasing the MLRS Weapon's Effectiveness
In 1986, the army awarded a contract for development of the M39 Army Tactical Missile System (ATACMS) Block I, intended to destroy targets at even longer ranges than the extended-range M26 rocket fired by the M270 MLRS. The ATACMS had a useful range of 62 miles, with the first production examples delivered to the army in 1991.

Each ATACMS is 13ft long, 2ft in diameter and weighs 3,687lb. Due to the rocket's size, an M270 MLRS can carry and launch only two ATACMS at a time. Each missile is in a sealed pod with the same external dimensions as the standard six-rocket M26 pod. Each Block I ATACMS carried 950 anti-personnel/anti-material submunitions. The Block II ATACMS carried only 275 submunitions, but the decreased payload tripled the weapon's range to 186 miles.

During Operation IRAQI FREEDOM, seventy-three M270 MLRS series vehicles fired a total of 857 M26 rockets and 414 ATACMSs. The latter could respond to a fire request within seven minutes by way of comparison; during Operation DESERT STORM, it had taken almost an hour for an ATACMS to respond to a fire request.

New MLRS Munitions
Due to rising costs the army ended the ATACMS program in 2007. Those remaining in the inventory went through a Service Life Extension Program (SLEP) in which the submunitions warheads of the older-generation ATACMS were replaced with unitary (no duds) blast fragmentation warheads.

The replacement for the ATACMS proved to be the M30 Guided Multiple Launch Rocket System (GMLRS) that first appeared in 2016. With a range of 43 miles, the M30 possesses greater accuracy with a much higher kill probability. In a 2016 issue of *Field Artillery* magazine appeared the following passage: 'The range, limited collateral damage and accuracy of GMLRS unitary rockets lend themselves not only to shaping and counterstrike roles, but also to close support. GMLRS unitary can impact safely within 200 meters [219 yards] of friendly forces – sometimes even closer, depending on the circumstances.'

The fielded variants in the GMLRS family of munitions included the Dual-Purpose Improved Conventional Munition (DPICM), the Alternative Warhead (AW) versions, meant to deal with area targets, and the Unitary version with a 200lb HE warhead to service point targets.

The third of the three munitions had its combat debut during Operation IRAQI FREEDOM. An extended range version went through testing in 2018, demonstrating a range of 86 miles. The following year, the army awarded a contract for production.

Precision Strike Missile

The planned replacement for the ATACMS and eventually the GMLRS is currently labeled the Precision Strike Missile (PrSM) Program and is under development. The expectation is that the PrSM will enter into production by 2023 if testing goes well. The PrSM will have a range of 54,560 yards (310 miles). Among the army's requirements for the PrSM will be that two will need to fit into the same launch pod that currently can hold only a single ATACMS.

In-flight, the PrSM must be able to locate its target despite heavy enemy electronic countermeasures and be more reliable than the ATACMS and GMLRS. Last but not least, the missile needs to have an open architecture

---

New Fire Support Team Vehicles

The replacement for the M981 FIST-V entered army service in 2000, based on the BFVs, the M3A3 Operation DESERT STORM version in particular. Updated with an array of the latest technologies such as an inertial navigation system, GPS and a Battlefield Combat Identification System (BCIS), the new vehicle became the M7 Bradley Fire Support Team (BFIST) Vehicle. Unlike the M981 FIST-V that had to halt to designate a target, the BFIST can acquire a target while on the move. The army's Stryker family of wheeled armored vehicles also has a FIST variant designated the M1131, which first appeared in service in 2002.

to support future improvements. Eventual plans call for the PrSM to have the ability to engage naval targets.

Wheeled MLRS

In 2000 the army acquired six vehicles for testing a new self-propelled rocket-launcher eventually designated the M142 High-Mobility Artillery Rocket System (HIMARS). The M142 consisted of a single six-tube rocket-launcher, the same type as used on the M270 MLRS series, mounted on the rear cargo bay of a 6 × 6 truck. Testing proved successful, and initial production examples entered US Army and Marine Corps' service in 2005.

Lieutenant Colonel Donald E. Gentry and Major Cullen G. Barbato of the XVIII Airborne Corps wrote the following in a January–February 1999 issue of *Field Artillery* magazine:

> HIMARS [High Mobility Artillery Rocket System] is a significant leap forward in fire support for early entry and light forces. Light force commanders who must deploy to undeveloped areas soon will have the firepower normally associated with heavier forces with the fielding of HIMARS early in the twenty-first century.

The HIMARS fires the same family of munitions as the M270 MLRS series, but carries only one pod of six rockets instead of the MLRS' two pods or twelve rockets or a single M39 ATACMS or GMLRS. The HIMARS computer fire control system allows for firing missions to be carried out in automatic or manual mode. Three HIMARS prototypes saw combat during Operation IRAQI FREEDOM in 2003, with production examples continuing to see productive employment throughout the Middle East and Afghanistan.

The HIMARS wheeled vehicle is much lighter at 24,000lb (12 tons) than the fully-tracked M270 MLRS series at 44,000lb (22 tons) and can be transported by the C-130 and C-17. For protection of the three-person crew, the transport truck has an armored cab. In total, the American military had 400 examples of the vehicle in service by 2011, with the goal of eventually acquiring 900 of them.

A New Towed 155mm Howitzer

Dissatisfaction with the weight of the towed M198 155mm howitzer at 15,722lb (about 8 tons) and numerous maintenance issues led to the army decision in the mid-1980s to search for a slimmed-down 155mm towed howitzer with much greater durability.

The leading candidate proved to be a proposed design by the Armaments Division of Vickers Shipbuilding and Engineering Limited (VSEL), which eventually became part of BAE Systems in 2004. They had conceived of a lightweight, towed 155mm howitzer that weighed half as much as the M198, using new materials such as titanium.

VSEL completed two prototypes in 1989 of its new 155mm howitzer. The firm originally referred to its prototypes as the 155mm ultra-light field howitzer (UFH). The American military designated these pre-production cannons the XM777 and, later, the XM777 Lightweight 155mm Howitzer (LW155).

The next step with the XM777 involved the British firm transferring manufacturing technology to the US. Two American-built pilot production howitzers appeared in 2002. Testing of these cannons convinced the DOD of the weapon's suitability for service, resulting in its fielding with both the US Army and Marine Corps in 2005 with the designation M777.

Description
The original M777 weighed in at 9,300lb (under 5 tons) and proved to be about 25 percent smaller than its predecessor, the M198. Due to its reduced weight and size compared to the M198, it can be towed into position by smaller vehicles and air-lifted by a greater variety of aerial platforms.

To improve the M777's firing accuracy and reaction time, an American firm under contract with BAE developed a towed artillery digitization (TAD) system for the cannon, which included GPS, an inertial navigation system, a radio and a Gun Display Unit (GDU). Entering service in 2006, the TAD-equipped M777s received the designation M777A1. The follow-on M777A2 version came with a software update allowing the cannon to fire the latest precision artillery rounds such as Excalibur.

Bradley Air Defense Systems
With the failures of the Cold War-era Sergeant York and other proposed AA vehicles, the army, as an interim measure, fielded the Bradley Stinger Fighting Vehicle (BSFV). It entailed replacing the infantrymen in the rear passenger compartment of either an M2 or M3 BFV with a two-man Stinger Missile Team. Their role was to exit the vehicle upon an aerial threat to the armored unit they were supporting and engage the enemy.

The downside of this scenario is the Stinger team would quickly find itself exposed to both indirect and direct enemy fire. Adding to the problem is the rest of the armored unit would have to either slow down or stop for the Stinger team until the firing engagement ended and the Stinger team re-embarked.

To correct the deficiencies of the BSFVs, in the summer of 1996 the army began testing the XM-6 Bradley Linebacker, envisioned for fielding in

1998. It consisted of a BFV having its TOW missile-launcher replaced by a four-round Stinger missile pod from the Avenger.

From an article in the January–February 1997 issue of *Air Defense* magazine is the following passage describing a portion of the vehicle: 'The Bradley Linebacker's slew-to-cue capabilities permit it to counter cruise missiles and makes it even more effective against both rotary and fixed-wing aircraft. The system's shoot-on-the-move capability and ability to engage targets at night give the task force commander 24-hour air defense coverage.'

Due to its focus on counter-insurgency operations in the Middle East, the army decided to strip all the Bradley Linebackers of their air defense components between 2006 and 2007, returning them to their original configurations. The army eventually envisioned fielding a much upgraded and more capable version of the Linebacker, but that proposed vehicle fell by the wayside.

Stryker Air Defense Vehicle

Instead of a new version of a Bradley air defense system, the army is planning on fielding by 2022 what will eventually amount to 144 examples of a new air-defense model of the Stryker family of wheeled vehicles. That vehicle acquired the label Interim Maneuver Short-Range Air Defense System (IM-SHORAD). The first version of the IM-SHORAD will have guns (30mm and 7.62mm) and missiles, Stinger and Hellfire.

The reason for the US Army's renewed emphasis on air defense appears in the following passage from the November–December 2019 issue of *Fires* magazine:

> ... opposing aircraft now present an enormous and immediate threat from both the information they gather for Fires [artillery] units and from their ability to provide close air-support or close combat attacks. These assets include rotary-wing aircraft, fixed-wing aircraft, tilt-rotors and unmanned aerial systems (UAS). This necessitates a robust air defense capability for modern troop formations that can tackle all aerial threats economically, especially proliferating drones such as quadcopters.

As time goes on, the army plans on fielding follow-on versions of the IM-SHORAD that will feature a directed energy weapon. The reasoning for use of a directed energy weapon appears in an October 2018 US Army news release quoting US Army Brigadier General Randall McIntire: '(Guns are) a relatively inexpensive solution. But it doesn't give us the range that we're seeing from our adversaries. We get range from our missiles, but they're becoming extraordinarily expensive ... Directed energy will be a complementary system to guns and missiles.'

Didn't Make the Cut

In 2001, the Marine Corps began thinking about taking the AIM-120 Advanced Medium-Range Air-to-Air Missile (AMRAM) employed by both the USAF and US Navy since 1991, and modifying it into a SAM. The goal was replacement of the aging Hawk SAM.

The army soon became interested in the possibility and had five proto-types built as a possible replacement for the Avenger. The launching plat-form of choice became the HMMWV (Humvee). On the rear cargo bay, a fixed in-place rack held four or more Surface-Launched Advanced Medium-Range Air-to-Air Missiles (SL-AMRAMs).

The 12ft-long missiles weighed 345lb and were radar-homing with inertial guidance. In flight, they reached a speed of Mach 4 (3,045mph). The missile-launching Humvees had no onboard radar and would have to depend on separate radar systems to detect and identify incoming aerial threats. Unfortunately, further development of the SL-AMRAM ended in 2005 due to a lack of funding.

Borrowing from the Navy

As a quick-fix solution to defend US Army installations located in combat zones from a variety of indirect fire weapons, there appeared in 2014 the Counter-Rocket, Artillery, Mortar (C-RAM) Intercept Land-Based Phalanx Weapon System (LPWS). It consists of a modified Navy Phalanx Close-In Weapon System (in service since 1980), mounted on a 35-ton semi-trailer towed by a tractor cab to its firing position.

To supplement its onboard search-and-track radar system, C-RAM also relies on other sensor systems connected to the weapon to aid it in detecting incoming enemy projectiles and then engaging them before they impact on their targets. The weapon system features a six-barrel M16A1 20mm Gatling gun (the same as that fitted to the Vulcan).

The weapon has a maximum rate of fire of up to 4,500 rounds per minute, with the typical engagement consuming around 300 rounds. The rounds themselves self-destruct beyond 2,187 yards (a little over 1 mile) to minimize collateral damage.

(**Below**) Starting in the late 1970s, the US Army began thinking about its inventory of M109s which had entered service in the early 1960s. The decision to either upgrade the M109 series or develop a new next-generation self-propelled 155mm howitzer proved a painful one. It wasn't until 1990 that the army adopted a much-modernized version of the M109 series seen here designated the M109A6 and nicknamed the 'Paladin'. (*Public domain*)

(**Opposite, above**) The Paladin retained the long-serving chassis of the M109 series as seen here, but came with a new larger turret to accommodate the latest technology, which included an inertial navigation system and a digitized fire-control system. These features allowed the vehicle to move quickly around the battlefield from one firing position to another, referred to as 'shoot-and-scoot'. That improved the Paladin's ability to avoid enemy counterbattery fire. (*Public domain*)

(**Below**) The key external design feature of the Paladin is the large storage bustle on the turret's rear, clearly visible in this photograph. The cannon on the vehicle went from 29ft to 35ft. The reason appears in an army 2019 press release: 'A longer barrel means that the explosion can have contact with the projectile for more time, increasing the pressure and then velocity of the round, which equals greater distances.' (*Richard and Barb Eshleman*)

(**Above**) Unlike the rounded corners on the front of the turret on earlier versions of the M109 series, the turret on the Paladin has a squared front. It is difficult but not impossible to discern in this photograph due to storage items around the turret. The vehicle had just entered into production when Operation DESERT STORM took place in 1991 so did not see action; but it did see combat during Operation IRAQI FREEDOM in 2003. (*Public domain*)

(**Opposite, above**) Inside the turret of the Paladin. The round just behind the cannon's breech is an inert training round, which is painted blue. The vehicle has a crew of four that can fire four rounds per minute for the first three minutes and one round per minute in sustained fire. There is onboard storage for thirty-nine rounds. The diesel-powered vehicle weighs approximately 34 tons and has a cruising range of 180 miles. (*Public domain*)

(**Opposite, below**) Until the early 1980s, the US Army's M109s depended on the M548, an unarmored vehicle based on the M113 series to re-supply them with ammunition. Beginning in 1982, the army began fielding the M992A2 Field Artillery Ammunition Supply Vehicle (FAASV) built on the armored chassis of the M109 series howitzer. Like the M109 series the FAASV series has been progressively upgraded, resulting in the suffixes A1 and now A2 being added to their designations. (*Public domain*)

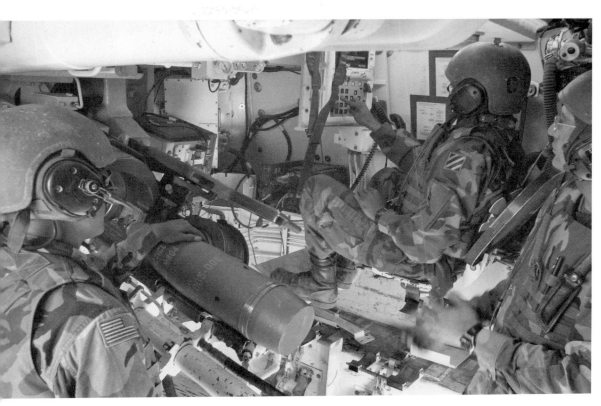

(**Opposite, above**) Pictured here are 155mm rounds, with their screwed-on fuzes visible. The M109 series' battlefield effectiveness has increased dramatically over the decades with advancements in its ammunition, such as precision-guided rounds like the M982 Excalibur 155 Extended-Range Artillery Projectile (ERAP). Such rounds aid in limiting collateral damage and permit effective engagement of point targets. (*Public domain*)

(**Opposite, below**) Replacing the light planes and helicopters employed by the US Army artillery branch for target acquisition is the AAI RQ-7 Shadow drone pictured here. It has a wingspan of 14ft and a length of 11ft 2in. Fully loaded, it weighs 375lb and has a range of 68 miles. With endurance of up to nine hours, with a top speed of 130mph and a cruising speed of 81mph, it can reach an altitude of 15,000ft. (*Public domain*)

(**Above**) In 1995, the US Army approved development of a new self-propelled 155mm howitzer, with a prototype delivered in 1999 which the service designated the XM2001 Crusader. Also, it would work together with a new ammunition re-supply vehicle based on the same chassis. The overall intention called for Crusader to replace the M109A6 Paladin and the M992 series (FAASV). Design issues and cost overruns resulted in its cancellation in 2002. Pictured here is the prototype Paladin. (*Chun-Lun Hsu*)

The US Army did not give up on its perceived need for a new self-propelled 155mm howitzer, and in 2000 development began on a family of eighteen vehicle variants using the same chassis, referred to as the Future Combat System (FCS). Among the variants was the XM1203 Non-Line-of-Sight Cannon (NLOS-C), with one of the eight prototypes built pictured here. Like the Crusader, the FCS foundered on a combination of design issues and cost overruns, leading to its cancellation in 2009. (*Public domain*)

The latest version of the M109 series is the M109A7 example pictured here during testing. From a US Army press release is a description of what this vehicle brings to the service: 'The program has leveraged Bradley commonality for key components – engine, trans-mission, final drive, and suspension – in a new hull. The new electric-gun drives and rammer components, as well as a microclimate air-conditioning system, will be powered by the common modular power system utilizing a 600-volt onboard electrical system in the existing cab and cannon assembly.' (*DOD*)

Beginning in 2000, the US Army began progressively upgrading its inventory of M270 Multiple Launch Rocket Systems, resulting in the introduction of the M270A1 and later the M270A2. For targets outside the range of the M26 rockets, the service fielded the Army Tactical Missile (ATACM) system, seen here fired from an M270 series MLRS. That missile would go on to be replaced in 2016 by the M30 Guided Multiple Launch Rocket System (GMLRS). *(Public domain)*

(**Above**) Operation DESERT STORM in 1991 clearly demonstrated to the US Army that the M901 Fire Support Team Vehicle (FIST-V) based on the M113 series of vehicles lacked the requisite mobility to keep up with the other vehicles in the army's inventory. These included the M1 Abrams series of tanks and the M2/M3 Bradley family of fighting vehicles. To resolve this issue, the army replaced the M901 with the M7 Bradley Fire Support Team (BFIST) vehicle seen here, beginning in 2000. (*BAE*)

(**Opposite, above**) In 2005, both the US Army and Marine Corps took into service the M142 High-Mobility Artillery Rocket System (HIMARS). It consisted of a single six-tube rocket-launcher, the same type as used on the M270 MLRS series, mounted on the rear cargo bay of a 6 × 6 truck, as pictured here. The vehicle is typically operated by a crew of three comprising the driver, gunner and section chief, although at a pinch a single soldier can work the weapon system. (*Public domain*)

(**Opposite, below**) Pictured here are several M777 155mm towed howitzers, a British-designed cannon license-built in the United States for both the US Army and the Marine Corps. It replaces the M198 155mm towed howitzer and began entering service in 2006. From a US Army press release on the weapon: 'The extensive use of titanium in all of its major structures makes the M777 7,000 pounds lighter than its predecessor with no sacrifice in range, stability, accuracy or mobility.' (*Public domain*)

(**Opposite, above**) An M777 at the moment of firing. As with most American military weapon systems, the M777 155mm towed howitzer went through various improvements to maintain its battlefield effectiveness. The latest version, the M777A2, has a Digital Fire Control System (DFCS), which includes an inertial navigation unit with a Global Positioning System (GPS) back-up, allowing it to immediately self-locate itself on the battlefield. The DFCS also consists of a mission computer, displays and digital communications capabilities. (*Public domain*)

(**Opposite, below**) Both smaller and lighter than its predecessor, the M198, the M777's smaller footprint and lower profile increases its strategic deployability and tactical mobility. It can be air-lifted by a variety of aerial platforms including helicopters, as seen in this picture of a Marine Corps CH-53E Sea Stallion. The US Army uses the CH-47D Chinook to move the cannon. Whereas the C-130 could only transport a single M198 at a time, it can accommodate two of the M777s. (*Public domain*)

(**Above**) As artillerymen have done for more than 100 years, a Marine cannoneer pulls the lanyard to his M777 155mm howitzer upon the order to fire. The crew of the piece can range from five to eight cannoneers, who can fire up to five rounds per minute for the first three minutes and after that, maintain a rate of fire of three rounds per minute. The weapon emplacement and ready-to-fire configuration takes place in just two minutes, and in almost the same amount of time, the weapon can be ready to move. (*Public domain*)

(**Above**) In 1995 the US Army asked industry to convert some of its M2A2 Bradley Infantry Fighting Vehicles (IFVs) into anti-aircraft vehicles by fitting them with the Stinger surface-to-air missile system and associated fire-control system from the AN/TWQ-1 Avenger based on the Humvee chassis. The result proved to be the M6 Linebacker pictured here. A single Stinger four-round missile pod from the Avenger replaced the standard two-round TOW missile launcher unit on the left-hand side of the vehicle's turret. (*Public domain*)

(**Opposite, above**) During the Iraqi insurrection, following Operation IRAQI FREEDOM, in 2003. The army found its most important installations under near-constant attack by the entire array of indirect-fire weapons including artillery, rockets and mortar rounds. To address this threat, the army fielded the Counter-Rocket, Artillery, Mortar (C-RAM) pictured here mounted on a semi-truck trailer. The main component of C-RAM is a version of the US Navy's radar-directed Phalanx Weapon Systems. (*Public domain*)

(**Opposite, below**) Unlike the US Navy's version of the Phalanx pictured, which fires tungsten armor-piercing (AP) rounds, the US Army's C-RAM version of the Phalanx fires the M940 Multi-Purpose (high-explosive-incendiary) Tracer (MPT-SD) round. The suffix letters 'SD' at the end of the ammunition's designation stand for self-destruct. If the round does not explode on impact with its intended target, it will explode on tracer burnout at 7,500ft. (*US Navy*)

Bibliography

Batchelor, John and Hogg, Ian, *Artillery* (New York, Charles Scribner's Sons, 1972).

Cole, Philip M., *Civil War Artillery at Gettysburg: Organization, Equipment, Ammunition and Tactics* (Cambridge, Da Capo Press, 2002).

Dastrup, Boyd L., *King of Battle: A Branch History of US Army's Field Artillery*, Training and Doctrine Command Branch History Series (Fort Monroe, VA., Office of the Command Historian, US Army Training and Doctrine Command, 1992).

Dastrup, Boyd L., *Modernizing the King of Battle, 1973–1991*, US Army Field Artillery Center and School Monograph Series (Fort Sill, Okla., Office of the Command Historian, US Army Field Artillery Center and School, 1994).

Dastrup, Boyd L., *Artillery Strong: Modernizing the Field Artillery for the 21st Century* (Combat Studies Institute Press, 2018).

Field Artillery in Military Operations Other Than War (Fort Leavenworth, Kan., Combat Studies Institute Press, 2004).

Gaujac, Paul, *American Field Artillery 1941–1945* (Paris, Histoire & Collections, 2009).

Gibbon, John, *The Artillerist Manual*, 1860 (Reprint, New York, Benchmark Publishers, 1970).

Hazlett, James C., Olmstead, Edwin and Hume Parks, M., *Field Artillery Weapons of the Civil War* (Newark, University of Delaware Press, 1983).

Hogg, Ian, *The Guns: 1939–1945* (New York, Ballantine Books, 1970).

Hogg, Ian, *A History of Artillery* (Middlesex, The Hamlyn Publishing Group Ltd, 1974).

Hogg, Ian, *The Illustrated Encyclopedia of Artillery* (London, Chartwell Books Inc., 1987).

Lewis, Emanuel Raymond, *Seacoast Fortifications of the United States: An Introductory History*, Rev. edition (Annapolis, Md., Leeward Publications, 1979).

Manucy, Albert, *Artillery Through the Ages* (Washington, Government Printing Office, 1949).

Mayo, Lida, *The Ordnance Department: On Beachhead and Battlefront* (Washington, D.C., Office of the Chief of Military History, United States Army, 1968).

McKenney, Janice E., *The Organizational History of the Field Artillery: 1775–2003* (Washington, D.C., US Army Center of Military History, 2007).

Ott, David E., *Field Artillery: 1954–1973* (Washington, Department of the Army, 1975).

Thomson, Harry C. and Mayo, Lida, *The Ordnance Department: Procurement and Supply* (Washington, Office of the Chief of Military History, US Army, 1960).

Williford, Glen M., *American Breechloading Mobile Artillery 1875–1953: An Illustrated Identification Guide* (PA, Schiffer Publishing Ltd, 2016).